Fountains In The Sand

Rambles Among The Oases Of Tunisia

Norman Douglas

Contents

Chapter I
EN ROUTE 7

Chapter II
BY THE OUED BAIESH 13

Chapter III
THE TERMID 18

Chapter IV
STONES OF GAFSA 23

Chapter V
SIDI ARMED ZARROUNG 28

Chapter VI
AMUSEMENTS BY THE WAY 35

Chapter VII
AT THE CAFE 40

Chapter VIII
POST-PRANDIAL MEDITATIONS 48

Chapter IX
SOME OF OUR GUESTS 52

Chapter X
THE OASIS OF LEILA 57

Chapter XI
A HAVEN OF REFUGE 65

Chapter XII
THE MYSTERIOUS COUNT 69

Chapter XIII
TO METLAOUI 77

Chapter XIV
PHOSPHATES 82

Chapter XV
   THE SELDJA GORGE 88
Chapter XVI
   AT THE HEAD OF THE WATERS 93
Chapter XVII
   ROMAN OLIVE-CULTURE 96
Chapter XVIII
   THE WORK OF PHILIPPE THOMAS 100
Chapter XIX
   OVER GUIFLA TO TOZEUR 105
Chapter XX
   A WATERY LABYRINTH 111
Chapter XXI
   OLD TISOUROS 116
Chapter XXII
   THE DISMAL CHOTT 120
Chapter XXIII
   THE GARDENS OF NEFTA 126
Chapter XXIV
   NEFTA AND ITS FUTURE 131

FOUNTAINS IN THE SAND

RAMBLES AMONG THE OASES OF TUNISIA

BY

Norman Douglas

FOUNTAINS
IN THE SAND

RAMBLES AMONG THE OASES OF TUNISIA

By Norman Douglas

Chapter I
EN ROUTE

Likely enough, I would not have remained in Gafsa more than a couple of days. For it was my intention to go from England straight down to the oases of the Djerid, Tozeur and Nefta, a corner of Tunisia left unexplored during my last visit to that country—there, where the inland regions shelve down towards those mysterious depressions, the Chotts, dried-up oceans, they say, where in olden days the fleets of Atlantis rode at anchor....

But there fell into my hands, by the way, a volume that deals exclusively with Gafsa—Pierre Bordereau's "La Capsa ancienne: La Gafsa moderne"—and, glancing over its pages as the train wound southwards along sterile river-beds and across dusty highlands, I became interested in this place of Gafsa, which seems to have had such a long and eventful history. Even before arriving at the spot, I had come to the correct conclusion that it must be worth more than a two days' visit.

The book opens thus: **One must reach Gafsa by way of Sfax.** Undoubtedly, this was the right thing to do; all my fellow-travellers were agreed upon that point; leaving Sfax by a night train, you arrive at Gafsa in the early hours of the following morning.

One must reach Gafsa by way of Sfax....

But a fine spirit of northern independence prompted me to try an alternative route. The time-table marked a newly opened line of railway which runs directly inland from the port of Sousse; the distance to Gafsa seemed shorter; the country was no doubt new and interesting. There was the station of Feriana, for instance, celebrated for its Roman antiquities and well worth a visit; I looked at the map and saw a broad road connecting this place with Gafsa; visions of an evening ride across the desert arose before my delighted imagination; instead of passing the night in an uncomfortable train, I should be already ensconced at a luxurious table d'hote, and so to bed.

The gods willed otherwise.

In pitch darkness, at the inhuman hour of 5.55 a.m., the train crept out of Sousse: sixteen miles an hour is its prescribed pace. The weather grew sensibly colder as we rose into the uplands, a stricken region, tree-less and water-less, with gaunt brown hills receding into the background; by midday, when Sbeitla was reached, it was blowing a hurricane. I had hoped to wander, for half an hour or so, among the ruins of this old city of Suffetula, but the cold, apart from their distance from the station, rendered this impossible; in order to reach the shed where luncheon was served, we were obliged to crawl backwards, crab-wise, to protect our faces from a storm which raised pebbles, the size of respectable peas, from the ground, and scattered them in a hail about us. I despair of giving any idea of that glacial blast: it was as if one stood, deprived of clothing, of skin and flesh—a jabbering anatomy—upon some drear Caucasian pinnacle. And I thought upon the gentle rains of London, from which I had fled to these sunny regions, I remembered the fogs, moist and warm and caressing: greatly is the English winter maligned! Seeing that this part of Tunisia is covered with the forsaken cities of the Romans who were absurdly sensitive in the matter of heat and cold, one is driven to the conclusion that the climate must indeed have changed since their day.

And my fellow-traveller, who had slept throughout the morning (we were the only two Europeans in the train), told me that this weather was nothing out of the common; that at this season it blew in such fashion for weeks on end; Sbeitla, to be sure, lay at a high point of the line, but the cold was no better at the present terminus, Henchir Souatir, whither he was bound on some business connected with the big phosphate company. On such occasions the natives barricade their doors and cower within over a warming-pan filled with the glowing embers of desert shrubs; as for Europeans—a dog's life, he said; in winter we are shrivelled to mummies, in summer roasted alive.

I spoke of Feriana, and my projected evening ride across a few miles of desert.

"Gafsa ... Gafsa," he began, in dreamy fashion, as though I had proposed a trip to Lake Tchad. And then, emphatically:

"*Gafsa?* Why on earth didn't you go over Sfax?"

"Ah, everybody has been suggesting that route."

"I can well believe it, Monsieur."

In short, my plan was out of the question; utterly out of the question. The road—a mere track—was over sixty kilometres in length and positively unsafe on a wintry night; besides, the land lay 800 metres in height, and a traveller would be frozen to death. I must go as far as Majen, a few stations beyond Feriana; sleep there in an Arab funduk (caravanserai), and thank my stars if I found any one willing to supply me with a beast for the journey onward next morning. There are practically no tourists along this line, he explained, and consequently no accommodation for them; the towns that one sees so beautifully marked on the map are railway stations—that and nothing more; and as to the broad highways crossing the southern parts of Tunisia in various directions—well, they simply don't exist, *voila*!

"That's not very consoling," I said, as we took our seats in the compartment again. "It begins well."

And my meditations took on a sombre hue. I thought of a little overland trip I had once undertaken, in India, with the identical object of avoiding a long circuitous railway journey—from Udaipur to Mount Abu. I remembered those "few miles of desert."

Decidedly, things were beginning well.

"If you go to Gafsa," he resumed, "—if you really propose going to Gafsa, pray let me give you a card to a friend of mine, who lives there with his family and may be useful to you. No trouble, I assure you!"

He scribbled a few lines, addressed to "Monsieur Paul Dufresnoy, Engineer," for which I thanked him. "We all know each other in Africa," he said. "It's quite a small place—our Africa, I mean. You could squeeze the whole of it into the Place de la Concorde.... Nothing but minerals hereabouts," he went on. "They talk and dream of them, and sometimes their dreams come true. Did you observe the young proprietor of the restaurant at Sbeitla? Well, a short time ago some Arabs brought him a handful of stones from the mountains; he bought the site for two or three hundred francs, and a company has already offered him eight hundred thousand for the rights of exploitation. Zinc! He is waiting till they offer a million."

Majen....

A solitary station upon the wintry plain—three or four shivering Arabs swathed in rags—desolation all around—the sun setting in an angry cloud. It was a strong impression; one realized, for the first time, one's distance from the life of civilized man. Night descended with the rush of a storm, and as the friendly train disappeared from my view, I seemed to have taken leave of everything human. This feeling was not lessened by my reception at the funduk, whose native manager sternly refused to give me that separate sleeping-room which, I had been assured, was awaiting me and which, as he truthfully informed me, was even then unoccupied. The prospect of passing the night with a crowd of Arabs was not pleasing.

Amiability being unavailing, I tried bribery, but found him adamantine.

I then produced a letter from the Resident of the Republic in Tunis, recommending me to all the ***bureaux indigenes*** of the country, my translation of it being confirmed and even improved upon, at the expense of veracity, by a spahi (native cavalryman) who happened to be present, and threatened the man with the torments of the damned if he failed to comply with the desires of his government.

"The Resident," was the reply, "is plainly a fine fellow. But he is not the ***ponsechossi***."

"Ponsechossi. What's that?"

"THIS," he said, excavating from under a pile of miscellaneous rubbish a paper whereon was displayed the official stamp of the ***Ponts et Chaussees***—the Department of Public Works for whose servants this choice apartment is—or rather ought to be—exclusively reserved: the rule is not always obeyed.

"Bring me THIS"—tapping the document proudly—"and you have the room."

"Could I at least find a horse in the morning—a mule—a donkey—a camel?"

"We shall see!" And he slouched away.

There was nothing to be done with the man. Your incorruptible Oriental is always disagreeable. Fortunately, he is rather uncommon.

But the excellent spahi, whom my letter from head-quarters had considerably impressed, busied himself meanwhile on my behalf, and at seven in the morning a springless, open, two-wheeled Arab cart, drawn by a moth-eaten old mule, was ready for my conveyance to Gafsa. In this instrument of torture were spent the hours from 7.30 a.m. to 4.30 p.m., memories of that ride being blurred by the physical discomfort endured. Over a vast plateau framed in distant mountains we were wending in the direction of a low gap which never came nearer; the road itself was full of deep ruts that caused exquisite agony as we jolted into them; the sun—a patch of dazzling light, cold and cheerless. At this hour, I reflected, the train from Sfax would already have set me down at Gafsa.

Save for a few stunted thorns in the moister places, the whole land, so far as the eye could reach, was covered with halfa-grass—leagues upon leagues of this sad grey-green desert reed. We passed a few nomad families whose children were tearing out the wiry stuff—it is never cut in Tunisia—which is then loaded on camels and conveyed to the nearest depot on the railway line, and thence to the seaboard. They were burning it here and there, to keep themselves warm; this is forbidden by law, but then—there is so much of it on these uplands, and the wind is so cold!

The last miles were easier travelling, as we had struck the track from Feriana on our left. Here, at an opening of the arid hills, where the road begins to descend in a broad, straight ribbon, there arose, suddenly, a distant glimpse of the oasis of Gafsa—a harmonious line of dark palm trees, with white houses and minarets in between. A familiar vision, and often described; yet one that never fails of its effect. A man may weary, after a while, of camels and bedouin maidens and all the picturesque paraphernalia of Arab life; or at least they end in becoming so trite that his eyes cease to take note of them; but there are two spectacles, ever new, elemental, that correspond to deeper impulses: this of palms in the waste—the miracle of water; and that of fire—the sun.

A low hill near the entrance of the town (it is marked Meda Hill on the map) had attracted my attention as promising a fine view. Thither, after settling my concerns at the hotel, I swiftly bent my steps; it was too late; the wintry sun had gone to rest. The oasis still lay visible, extended at my feet; on the other side I detected, some three miles away, a white spot—a house, no doubt—standing by a dusky patch of palms that rose solitary out of the stones. Some subsidiary oasis, probably; it looked an interesting place, all alone there, at the foot of those barren hills.

And still I lingered, my only companion being a dirty brown dog, of the jackal type, who walked round me suspiciously and barked, or rather whined, without ceasing. At last I took up a stone, and he ran away. But the stone remained in my hand; I glanced at it, and saw that it was an implement of worked flint. Here was a discovery! Who were these carvers of stones, the aboriginals of Gafsa? How lived they? A prolonged and melodious whistle from the distant railway station served to remind me of the gulf of ages that separates these prehistoric men from the life of our day.

But as if to efface without delay that consoling impression, my downward path led past a dark cavern before which was lighted a fire that threw gleams into its recesses; there was a family crouching around it; they lived in the hollow rock. A high-piled heap of bones near at hand suggested cannibalistic practices.

These, then, are the primitives of Gafsa. And for how long, I wonder, has this convenient shelter been inhabited? From time immemorial, perhaps; ever since the days of those others. And, after all, how little have they changed in the intervening thousands of years! The wild-eyed young wench, with her dishevelled hair, ferocious bangle-ornaments, tattooings, and nondescript blue rags open at the side and revealing charms well fitted to disquiet some robust savage—what has such a creature in common with the rest of us? Not even certain raptures, misdeemed primeval; hardly more than what falls to man and beast alike. On my appearance, she rose up and eyed me unabashed; then sank to the ground again, amid her naked and uncouth cubs; the rock, she said, was warmer than the black tents; they paid no rent; for the rest, her man would return forthwith. And soon there was a clattering of stones, and a herd of goats scrambled up and vanished within the opening.

The partner was neither pleased nor displeased at seeing me there; every day he went to pasture his flock on the slopes of the opposite Jebel Guetter, returning at nightfall; he tried to be civil but failed, for want of vocabulary. I gave him the salutation, and passed on in the gloaming.

Chapter II
BY THE OUED BAIESH

This collecting of flint implements grows upon one at Gafsa; it is in the air. And I find that quite a number of persons have anticipated me in this amusement, and even written tomes upon the subject—it is ever thus, when one thinks to have made a scientific discovery. These stones are scattered all over the plain, and Monsieur Couillault has traced the site of several workshops—*ateliers*—of prehistoric weapons near Sidi Mansur, which lies within half a mile of Gafsa, whence he has extracted—or rather retrieved, for the flints merely lie upon the ground—quantities of instruments of every shape; among them, some saws and a miniature spade.

My collection of these relics, casually picked up here and there, already numbers two hundred pieces, and illustrates every period of those early ages—uncouth battle-axes and spear-points; fine needles, apparently used for sewing skins together; the so-called laurel-leaves, as thin as card-board; knife-blades; instruments for scraping beast-hides—all of flint. What interests me most, are certain round throwing-stones; a few are flat on both sides, but others, evidently the more popular shape, are flat below and rise to a cone above. Of these latter, I have a series of various sizes; the largest are for men's hands, but there are smaller ones, not more than eleven centimetres round, for the use of children: one thinks of the fierce little hands that wielded them, these many thousand years ago. Even now the natives will throw by preference with a stone of this disk-like shape—the cone pointing downwards. But, judging by the size of their implements, the hands of this prehistoric race can hardly have been as large as those of their modern descendants.

Then, as now, Gafsa must have been an important site; the number of these weapons is astonishing. Vast populations have drifted down the stream of time at this spot, leaving no name or mark behind them, save these relics fashioned, by the merest of chances, out of a practically imperishable material; steel and copper would have rotted away long ago, and the stoutest palaces crumbled to dust under the teeth of the desert air.

The bed of the Oued Baiesh, which flows past Gafsa and is nearly half a mile broad in some places, is rich in these worked flints which have been washed out of its steep banks by the floods. Walking here the other day with a miserable young Arab who, I verily believe, had attached himself to me out of sheer boredom (since he never asked for a sou), I observed, in the distance, a solitary individual, a European, pacing slowly along as though wrapped in meditation; every now and then he bent down to the ground.

"That's a French gentleman from Gafsa. He collects those stones of yours all day long."

Another amateur, I thought.

"But not like yourself," he went on. "He picks them up, bad and good, and when they don't look nice he works at them with iron things; I've seen them! He makes very pretty stones, much prettier than yours. Then he sends them away."

"How do you know this?"

"I've looked in at his window."

A modern "atelier" of flints—this was an amusing revelation. Maybe—who knows?—half the museums of Europe are stocked with these superior products.

Sages will be interested to learn that Professor Koken, of Tuebingen, in a learned pamphlet, lays it down that these flints of Gafsa belong to the Mesvinian, Strepyian, Praechellean—to say nothing of the Mousterian, Aurignacian, Solutrean, Magdalenian, and other types. So be it. He further says, what is more intelligible to the uninitiated, that a bed of hard conglomerate which crops up at Gafsa on either side of the Oued Baiesh, has been raised in days of yore; it was raised so slowly that the river found time to carve itself a bed through it during the process of elevation; nevertheless, a certain class of these artificial implements, embedded since God knows when, already formed part of this natural conglomerate ere it began to uplift itself. This will give some idea of the abysm of time that lies between us and the skin-clad men that lived here in olden days.

An abysm of time...

But I remembered the cave-wench of the Meda Hill. And my companion to-day was of the same grade, a characteristic semi-nomad boy of the poorest class; an orphan, of course (they are nearly all orphans), and quite abandoned. His whole vocabulary could not have exceeded one hundred and fifty words; he had never heard of the Apostle of Allah or his sacred book; he could only run, and throw stones, and endure, like a beast, those ceaseless illnesses of which only death, an early death as a rule, is allowed to cure them. His clothing was an undershirt and the inevitable burnous, brown with dirt.

"What have you done to-day?" I asked him.

"Nothing."

"And yesterday?"

"Nothing. Why should I do anything?"

"Don't you *ever* wash?"

"I have nobody to wash me."

Yet they appreciate the use of unguents. The other day a man accidentally poured a glassful of oil into the dusty street. Within a moment a crowd of boys were gathered around, dabbling their hands into it and then rubbing them on their hair; those that possessed boots began by ornamenting them, and thence conveyed the stuff to their heads—the ground was licked dry in a twinkling; their faces glistened with the greasy mixture. "That's good," they said.

Such, I daresay, were the pastimes of those prehistoric imps of the throwing-disks, and their clothing must have been much the same.

For what is the burnous save a glorified aboriginal beast-skin? It has the same principle of construction; the major part covers the human back and sides; the beast's head forms the hood; where the forefeet meet, the thing is tied together across the breast, leaving a large open slit below, and a smaller one above, where the man's head emerges.

The character of the race is summed up in that hopeless garment, which unfits the wearer for every pleasure and every duty of modern life. An article of everyday clothing which prevents a man from using his upper limbs, which swathes them up, like a silkworm in its cocoon—can anything more insane be imagined? Wrapped therein for nearly all their lives, the whole race grows round-shouldered; the gastric region, which ought to be protected in this climate of extremes, is exposed; the heating of their heads, night and day, with its hood, cannot but injure their brains; their hands become weak as those of women, with claw-like movements of the fingers and an inability to open the palm to the full.

No wonder it takes ten Arabs to fight one negro; no wonder their spiritual life is apathetic, unfruitful, since the digits that explore and design, following up the vagrant fancies of the imagination, are practically atrophied. You will see beggars who find it too troublesome, on cold days, to extricate their hands for the purpose of demanding alms! Man has been described as a tool-making animal, but the burnous effectually counteracts that wholesome tendency; it is a mummifying vesture, a step in the direction of fossilification. Will the natives ever realize that the abolition of this sleeveless and buttonless anachronism is one of the conditions of their betterment? Have *they* made the burnous, or vice-versa? No matter. They came together somehow, and suited one another.

The burnous is the epitome of Arab inefficiency.

They call it simple, but like other things that go by that name, it defeats it own objects of facilitating the common operations of life. It is amusing to watch them at their laundry-work. Unless a man stand still and upright, the end of this garment is continually slipping down from his shoulders; one of the washerman's hands, therefore, is employed in holding it in its place; the other grasps a stick upon which he leans while stamping a war-dance with his feet upon the linen. This is only half the performance, for a friend, holding up *his* cloak with one hand, must bend over and ladle the necessary water upon the linen with the other. Thus two men are requisitioned to wash a shirt—a hand of one, two feet of the other. No wonder they do not wash them often; the undertaking, thanks to the burnous, is too complicated.

Yet there is no denying that it adds charm to the landscape; it is highly decorative; its colour and shape and peculiar texture are as pleasing to the beholder as must have been the toga of the old Romans (which, by the way, was a purely ceremonial covering, to be doffed during work: so Cincinnatus, when the senators found him at the plough, went in to dress in his toga ere receiving them).

Stalking along on their thin bare shanks, their glittering eyes and hooked noses shaded within its hood, many adult Arabs assume a strangely bird-like appearance; while the smooth-faced youths, peering from under its coquettish folds, remind one of third-rate actresses out for a spree. In motion, when some half-naked boy sits merrily upon a galloping stallion, his bare limbs and flying burnous take on the passionate grace of a panathenaic frieze; it befits equally well the repose of old age, crouching at some street-corner in hieratic immobility.

Yes, there is no denying that it looks artistic; the burnous is picturesque, like many antediluvian things. And of course, where nothing better can be procured, it will protect you from the cold and the stinging rays of the sun. But if a European wants a chill in the liver or any other portion of the culinary or postprandial department, he need only wear one for a few days on end; raise the hood, and you will have a headache in ten minutes.

Nevertheless I have bought one, and am wearing it at this very moment. But not as the poorer Arabs do. Beneath it there is a suit of ordinary winter clothing, as well as two English ulsters—and this ***indoors***. Perhaps this will give some idea of the cold of Gafsa. There is no heating these bare rooms with their icy walls and floorings: out of doors a blizzard is raging that would flay a rhinoceros. And the wind of Gafsa has this peculiarity, that it is equally bitter from whichever point of the compass it blows. Let those who contemplate the supreme madness of coming to the sunny oasis at the present season of the year (January) bring not only Arctic vestment, eiderdowns, fur cloaks, carpets and foot-warmers, but also, and chiefly, efficient furnaces and fuel for them.

For such things seem to be unknown hereabouts.

Chapter III
THE TERMID

The chief attractions of Gafsa, beside the oasis, are the tall minaret with its prospect over the town and plantations, and the Kasbah or fortress, a Byzantine construction covering a large expanse of ground and rebuilt by the French on theatrical lines, with bastions and crenellations and other warlike pomp; thousands of blocks of Roman masonry have been wrought into its old walls, which are now smothered under a modern layer of plaster divided into square fields, to imitate solid stonework. It looks best in the moonlight, when this childish cardboard effect is toned down.

One of the two hot springs of Gafsa is enclosed within this Kasbah, while the other rises near at hand and flows into the celebrated baths—the ***termid***, as the natives, using the old Greek word, still call it. It is a large and deep stone basin, half full of warm water, in which small fishes, snakes and tortoises disport themselves; the massive engirdling walls demonstrate its Roman origin. Thick mists hang over the ***termid*** in the early mornings, when the air is chilly, but later on it becomes a lively place, full of laughter and splashings. Here, for a sou, you may get the boys to jump down from the parapet and wallow among the muddy ooze at the bottom; the liquid, though transparent, is not colourless, but rather of the blue-green tint of the aquamarine crystal; it flows rapidly, and all impurities are carried away.

There are always elderly folk idling about these premises, and youngsters with rods tempting the fish out of the water; day after day the game goes on, the foolish creatures nibble at the bait and are drawn up on high; their fellows see the beginning of the tragedy, but never the end, where, floundering in the street, the victims cover their silvery scales with a coating of dust and expire ignominiously, as unlike live fishes as if they came ready cooked out of the kitchen *panes et frits*.

Above this basin is another one, that of the women; and below it, at the foot of a lurid stairway, a suite of subterranean (Roman) chambers, a kind of Turkish bath for men, where the water hurries darkly through; the place is reeking with a steamy heat, and objectionable beyond words; it would not be easy to describe, in the language of polite society, those features in which it is most repulsive to Europeans.

How easily, as in former days, might now a health-giving wonder be created out of these waters of Gafsa, that well up in a river of warmth and purity, only to be hopelessly contaminated! The French tried the experiment, but the natives objected, and they gave way: these are the spots on the sunny ideal of "pacific penetration." Any other nationality—while allowing the Arabs a fair share of the element—would simply have rebuilt this *termid* and put it to a decent use, in the name of cleanliness and civilization; the natives acquiescing, as they always do when they recognize their masters. Or, if a display of force was considered inadvisable, why not try the *suaviter in modo*? Had a couple of local saints been judiciously approached, the population would soon have discovered that the *termid* waters are injurious to health and only fit for unbelievers. What is the use of a *marabout*, if he cannot be bribed?

I am all for keeping up local colour, even when it entails, as it generally does, a certain percentage of local smells; yet it seems a pity that such glorious hot springs, a gift of the gods in a climate like this, should be converted into a *cloaca maxima*, especially in Gafsa, which already boasts of a superfluity of open drains.

But my friend the magistrate showed me a special bathing room which has lately been built for the use of Europeans. We tried the door and found it locked.

Where was the key?

At the *Ponts et Chaussees*.

Thither I went, and discovered an elderly official of ample proportions dozing in a trim apartment—the chief of the staff. Great was this gentleman's condescension; he bade me be seated, opened his eyes wide, and enquired after my wants.

The key? The key of the *piscine?* He regretted he could give me no information as to its whereabouts—no information whatever. He had never so much as seen the key in question; perhaps it had been lost, perhaps it never existed. Several tourists, he added, had already come on the same quest as myself; he also, on one occasion last year, thought he would like to take a bath, but—what would you? There was no key! If I liked to bathe, I might go to the tank at the gardens of Sidi Ahmed Zarroung.

I gently insisted, pointing out that I did not care for a walk across the windswept desert only to dip myself into a pool of lukewarm and pestilentially sulphureous water. But "the key" was evidently a sore subject.

"There is no key, Monsieur"; and he accompanied the words with a portentous negative nod that blended the resigned solicitude of an old and trusted friend with the firmness of a Bismarck. This closed the discussion; with expressions of undying gratitude, and a few remarks as to the palpable advantages to be derived from keeping a public bathing-room permanently locked, I left him to his well-earned slumbers....

It is hard to understand what the guide-books mean when they call the market of Gafsa "rich and well-appointed": a five-pound note, I calculate, would buy the entire exhibition. The produce, though varied, is wretched; but the scenery fine. Over a dusty level, strewn with wares, you look upon a stretch of waving palms, with the distant summit of Jebel Orbata shining in the deep blue sky. Here are a few butchers and open-air cooks who fry suspicious-looking bundles of animal intestines for the epicurean Arabs; a little saddlery; half a camel-load of corn; a broken cart-wheel and rickety furniture put up to auction; one or two halfa-mats of admirable workmanship; grinding-stones; musty pressed dates, onions, huge but insipid turnips and other green things, red peppers——

Those peppers! An adult Arab will eat two pounds of them a day. I have seen, native women devouring, alternately, a pepper, then a date, then another pepper, then another date, and so on, for half an hour. An infant at the breast, when tired of its natural nourishment, is often given one of these fiery abominations to suck, as an appetizer, or by way of change and amusement. Their corroding juices are responsible for half the stomach troubles of the race; a milk diet would work wonders as a cure, if the people could be induced to do things by halves; but they cannot; it is "all peppers or all milk," and, the new diet disagreeing with them at first, they return to their peppers and a painful disease.

It is this lack of measure and reasonableness among them which accounts for what I believe to be a fact, namely, that there are more reclaimed drunkards among

Arabs than among ourselves. They will break off the alcohol habit violently, and for ever. And this they do not out of principle, but from impulse or, as they prefer to call it, inspiration; indeed, they regard our men of fixed principles as weaklings and cowards, who stiffen themselves by artificial rules because they cannot trust their judgments to deal with events as they arise—(the Arab regards terrestrial life as a chain of accidents)—cowards and infidels, trying to forestall by human devices the unascertainable decrees of Allah.

Allah wills it! That is why they patiently bear the extremes of hunger, and why, if fortune smiles, they gorge like Eskimos, like boa-constrictors.

I have seen them so distended with food as to be literally incapable of moving. Only yesterday, there swept past these doors a bright procession, going half-trot to a lively chant of music: the funeral of a woman. I enquired of a passer-by the cause of her death.

"She ate too much, and burst."

During the summer months, in the fruit-growing districts, quite a number of children will "burst" in this fashion every day.

Mektoub! the parents then exclaim. It was written.

And no doubt there is such a thing as a noble resignation; to defy fate, even if one cannot rule it. Many of us northerners would be the better for a little ***mektoub***. But this doctrine of referring everything to the will of Allah takes away all stimulus to independent thought; it makes for apathy, improvidence, and mental fossilification. A creed of everyday use which hampers a man's reasoning in the most ordinary matters of life—is it not like a garment that fetters his hands?

Mektoub is the intellectual ***burnous*** of the Arabs....

There is some movement, at least, in this market; often the familiar story-tellers, surrounded by a circle of charmed listeners; sometimes, again, a group of Soudanese from Khordofan or Bournu, who parade a black he-goat, bedizened with gaudy rags because devoted to death; they will slay him in due course at some shrine; but not just now, because there is still money to be made out of his ludicrous appearance, with an incidental dance or song on their own part. Vaguely perturbing, these negro melodies and thrummings; their reiteration of monotony awakens tremulous echoes on the human diaphragm and stirs up hazy, primeval mischiefs.

And this morning there arrived a blind singer, or bard; he was led by two boys, who accompanied his extemporaneous verses—one of them tapping with a pebble on an empty sardine-tin, while the other belaboured a beer-bottle with a rusty nail: both solemn as archangels; there was also a professional accompanist, who screwed his mouth awry and blew sideways into a tall flute, his eyes half-closed in ecstatic rapture. Arab gravity never looks better than during inanely grotesque performances of this kind; in such moments one cannot help loving them, for these are the little episodes that make life endurable.

The music was not altogether original; it reminded me, with its mechanical punctuations, of a concerto by Paderewski which contains an exquisite movement between the piano and kettledrum—since the flute, which ought to have supported the voice, was apparently dumb, although the artist puffed out his cheeks as if his life depended upon it. Only after creeping quite close to the performers could I discern certain wailful breathings; this brave instrument, all splotched with variegated colours, gave forth a succession of anguished and asthmatic whispers, the very phantom of a song, like the wind sighing through the branches of trees.

Chapter IV
STONES OF GAFSA

There are interesting walks in the neighbourhood of Gafsa, but I can imagine nothing more curious than the town itself; a place of some five thousand inhabitants, about a thousand of whom are Jews, with a sprinkling of Italian tradespeople and French officials and soldiers. Beyond naming the streets and putting up a few lamps, the Government has left it in its Arab condition; the roadways are unpaved, hardly a single wall is plumb; the houses, mostly one-storied, lean this way and that, and, being built of earthen-tinted sun-dried brick, have an air of crumbling to pieces before one's very eyes. A heavy and continuous shower would be the ruin of Gafsa; the structures would melt away, like that triple wall of defence, erected in medieval times, of which not a vestige remains. Yet the dirt is not as remarkable as in many Eastern places, for every morning a band of minor offenders is marched out of prison by an overseer to sweep the streets. Sometimes an upper room is built to overlook, if possible, the roadway; it is supported on palm-rafters, forming a kind of tunnel underneath. Everywhere are immense blocks of chiselled stone worked into the ephemeral Arab clay as doorsteps or lintels, or lying about at random, or utilized as seats at the house entrance; they date from Roman or earlier times—columns, too, some of them adorned with the lotus-pattern, the majority unpretentious and solid.

What do the natives think of these relics of past civilization? Do they ever wonder whence they came or who made them? "The stones are there," they will tell you. Yet the wiser among them will speak of ***Ruman***; they have heard of ***Ruman*** moneys and antiquities.

Arabs have a saying that Gafsa was founded by Nimrod's armour-bearer; but a more reasonable legend, preserved by Orosius and others, attributes its creation to Melkarth, the Libyan and Tyrian Hercules, hero of colonization. He surrounded it with a wall pierced by a hundred gates, whence its presumable name, Hecatompylos, the city of a hundred gates. The Egyptians ruled it; then the Phoenicians, who called it Kafaz—the walled; and after the destruction of Carthage it became the retreat and treasure-house of Numidian kings. Greeks, too, exercised a powerful influence on the place, and all these civilized peoples had prepared Gafsa to appreciate the beneficent rule of the Romans.

Then came Vandals and Byzantines, who gradually grew too weak to resist the floods of plundering Arab nomads; the rich merchants fled, their palaces fell to ruins; the town became a collection of mud huts inhabited by poor cultivators who lived in terror of the neighbouring Hammama tribe of true Arabs, that actually forbade them to walk beyond the limits of the Jebel Assalah—a couple of miles distant. So the French found them in 1881.

There are, however, a few decent houses, two-storied and spacious; in one of them, I am told, lives the family of Monsieur Dufresnoy, to whom my fellow traveller at Sbeitla gave me a card. He is absent at the Metlaoui mines just now, and his wife and children in Paris.

The cleansing of the streets by prisoners does not extend to the native houses and courtyards, which therefore survive in all their original, inconceivable squalor—squalor so uncompromising that it has long ago ceased to be picturesque. What glimpses into humble interiors, when native secretiveness has not raised a rampart of earthen bricks at the inside of the entrance! In the daytime it is like looking into vast, abandoned pigsties, fantastically encumbered with palm-logs, Roman building-blocks and rubbish-heaps which display the accumulated filth of generations—there is hardly a level yard of ground—rags and dust and decay! Here they live, the poorer sort, and no wonder they have as little sense of home as the wild creatures of the waste. But at night, when the most villainous objects take on mysterious shapes and meanings, these courtyards become grand; they assume an air of biblical desolation, as though the curse of Heaven had fallen upon the life they once witnessed; and even as you look into them, something stirs on the ground: it is an Arab, sleeping uneasily in his burnous; he has felt, rather than heard, your presence, and soon he unwinds his limbs and rises out of the dust, like a sheeted ghost.

It is an uncanny gift of these folks to come before you when least expected; to be ever-present, emerging, one might almost say, out of the earth. Go to the wildest corner of this thinly populated land, and you may be sure that there is an Arab, brooding among the rocks or in the sand, within a few yards of you.

The stones are there. This is another feature which they have in common with the beasts of the earth: never to pause before the memorials of their own past. Goethe says that where men are silent, stones will speak. If ever they spoke, it is among these crumbling, composite walls of Gafsa.

A Roman inscription of the age of Hadrian, which now forms the step of an Arab house, will arrest your glance and turn your thoughts awhile in the direction of this dim, romantic figure. How little we really know of the Imperial wanderer, whose journeyings may still be traced by the monuments that sprang up in his footsteps! Never since the world began has there been a traveller in the grandiose style of Hadrian; he perambulated his world like a god, crowned with a halo of benevolence and omnipotence.

And it occurs to me that there must be other relics of antiquity still buried under the soil of Gafsa, which is raised on a mound, like an island, above the surrounding country; particularly in the vicinity of the ***termid***, which we may suppose to have lain near the centre of the old town. And where are the paving-stones? The painstaking John Leo says that the streets of Gafsa are "broad and paved, like those of Naples or Florence." Have they been slowly submerged under the debris of Arabism, or taken up and worked into the masonry of the Kasbah and other buildings? Not one is left: so much is certain.

I borrowed Sallust and tried to press some flavour out of his description of Marius' march to the capture of Gafsa. It was a fine military performance, without a doubt; he led his troops by unsuspected paths across the desert, fell upon the palace, sacked and burnt it, and divided the booty among his soldiers: all this without the loss of a single man. The natives needed a lesson, and they got it; to this day the name of Marius is whispered among the black tents as that of some fabulous hero. But what interests me most is the style of Sallust himself. How ultra-modern this historian reads! His outlook upon life, his choice of words, are the note of tomorrow; and when I compare with him certain writers of the Victorian epoch, I seem to be unrolling a papyrus from Pharaoh's tomb, or spelling out the elucubrations of some maudlin scribe of Prester John.

The stones are there. And the quarries whence the Romans drew them have also been found, by Guerin; they lie in the flanks of the Jebel Assalah, and are well worth a visit; legions of bats— *tirlils*, the Arabs call them—hang in noisome clusters from the roof.

Concerning these bats, the following story is told in Gafsa.

Not long ago a rich Englishman came here. He used to go out in the evenings and shoot bats; then he put them into bottles with spirits of wine—he was an amateur of bats. On the day of his departure from the place, he said to the polyglot Arab guide whom he had picked up somewhere on his wanderings:

"You will rejoin me in Tunis in ten days. Bring me more bats—tirlils: **comprenni?**—from this country. I will give you fifty centimes apiece."

"Bon, Monsieur," said the guide, and took counsel with the folks of Gafsa, who, after certain reservations and stipulations, showed him the way into these quarries.

On the day appointed he entered the rich tourist's hotel in Tunis, followed by ten porters, each carrying a large sack.

"Hallo!" said the Englishman, "what's all this?"

"Bats, Monsieur."

"Eh? How much?"

"Bats; *tirlils*, *chauve-souris*, *pipistrelli*... They will need much bottles. Six hundred tirlils in each sack; ten sacks; six thousand tirlils. Much bottles! Three thousand francs, Monsieur. Shall I open him?"

The tourist cast a dismayed glance over the sacks, gently heaving with life.

"Look here," he said, "I'll give you fifty francs...."

The Arab was surprised and grieved. He thought he was giving a pleasure to Monsieur, who had asked for bats. He had been obliged to borrow money from his aged mother to help to pay the nine hundred francs which he had already disbursed for assistance in catching the tirlils; he had risked his life; there were the transport expenses, too: very heavy. He had travelled with many Englishmen and had always found them to be men of honour—men who kept their word. And in this case there were witnesses to the bargain, who would be ready, if necessary, to go into the French tribunals and testify to what they had heard....

"I see. Well, come to-morrow morning, but go away now, quick! before I break your head. Take your damned tirlils to your damned funduk, and be off!—clear out!—*comprenni?*"

And he looked so very angry that the Arab, a prudent fellow, walked backwards out of the room, more surprised and grieved than ever.

Thanks to the disinterested and strenuous exertions of a Jewish international lawyer, the affair was settled out of court after all—fifteen hundred francs, plus expenses of transport.

Chapter V
SIDI AHMED ZARROUNG

Sidi Ahmed Zarroung—that is the name of the miniature oasis visible from the Meda Hill, at the foot of those barren slopes. It is a pleasant afternoon's walk from Gafsa.

The intervening plain is encrusted with stones—stones great and small. Here and there are holes in the ground, where the natives have unearthed some desert shrub for the sake of its roots which, burnt as fuel, exhale a pungent odour of ammonia that almost suffocates you. Once the water-zone of Gafsa is passed, every trace of cultivation vanishes. And yet, to judge by the number of potsherds lying about, houses must have stood here in days of old. An Arab geographer of the eleventh century says that there are over two hundred flourishing villages in the neighbourhood of Gafsa; and Edrisius, writing a century later, extols its prosperous suburbs, and pleasure-houses.

Where are they now?

One of these villages, surely, must have lain near this fountain of Sidi Ahmed Zarroung, which now irrigates a few palms and vegetables and then loses itself in the sand; a second spring, sulphureous and medicinal, but destructive to plants, rises near at hand. This is the one which the gentleman of the **Ponts et Chaussees** recommended me for bathing purposes.

But I saw no trace of ancient life here; there is only a muddy pond, full of amorous frogs and tortoises, cold-blooded beasts, but fiery in their passions; and a few Arabs that live in the large white house, or camp on the plain around. They told me that the descendants of the holy man who gave his name to the place are still alive, but they knew nothing of his history beyond this, that he was very pious indeed.

If you do not mind a little scrambling, you can climb from here up to the last spur of the Jebel Guettor which overlooks the plain—it is crowned by a ruined building, once whitewashed, and easily visible from Gafsa. On its slopes I struck a vein of iron, another of those scientific discoveries, no doubt, like the flint implements, in which someone else will have anticipated me. And here I also found iron in a more civilized shape, a fragment of a shell—relic, perhaps, of the first French expedition against Gafsa, or of some more recent artillery practice.

From its summit one sees the configuration of the country as on a map; the high Jebel Orbata, 1170 metres, now covered with snow, coming forward to meet you on the other side of the wide valley. From this point it is easy to realize, as did the commander of that French expedition, the significance of this speck of culture, its strategic value: Gafsa is a veritable key to the Sahara. I daresay the abundant water-supply of the town is due to these two chains of hills which almost touch each other and so force the water to rise from its underground bed.

At this elevation you perceive that Gafsa is truly a hill-oasis, bleak mountains rising up on all sides save the south. There, where the two highest ranges converge from east and west, where the broad waterway of the Oued Baiesh has in olden days, when it wandered with less capricious flow, carved itself a channel through the opening—there, at the very narrowest point—sits the oasis. A tangle of palms that sweep southward in a radiant trail of green, the crenellated walls of the Kasbah gleaming through the interstices of the foliage—the whole vision swathed in an orange-tawny frame of desolation, of things non-human....

I was tempted to think that the sunset view from the Meda eminence was the finest in the immediate neighbourhood of Gafsa. Not so; that from the low hills behind Sidi Mansur, with the stony ridge of Jebel Assalah at your back, surpasses it in some respects. Through a gap you look towards the distant green plantations, with a shimmering level in the foreground; on your other side lies the Oued Baiesh, crossed by the track to Kairouan, where strings of camels are for ever moving to and fro, laden with merchandise from the north or with desert products from the oases of Djerid and Souf. The dry bed of the torrent glows in hues of isabel and cream, while its perpendicular mud-banks, on the further side, gleam like precipices of amber; the soil at your feet is besprinkled with a profusion of fair and fragile flowerlets.

Here stand, like sentinels at the end of all things living, the three or four last, lonely palms—they and their fellows lower down are fed by a silvery streamlet which is forced upwards, I suppose, by contact with Professor Koken's conglomerate; above and below this oasis-region the river-bed is generally dry. It must be a wonderful sight, however, when the place is in flood—a deluge of liquid ooze careering madly southward towards the dismal Chotts amid the crashing of stones and palm trees and the collapse of banks. For the Oued Baiesh can be angry at times; in 1859 it submerged fifty hectares of the Gafsa gardens.

Instead of returning by the main road from Sidi Mansur, one can bend a little to the right and so pass the military hospital, a large establishment which looks as if it could be converted into a barrack in case of need. This is as it should be. Gafsa is a rallying-point, and must be prepared for emergencies. Here, too, lie the cemeteries: the Jewish, fronting the main road, with a decent enclosure; that of the Christians, framed in a wire fence and containing a few wooden crosses, imitation broken columns and tinsel wreaths; Arab tombs, scattered over a large undefined tract of brown earth, and clustering thickly about some white-domed maraboutic monument, whose saintly relics are desirable companionship for the humbler dead.

The bare ground here is littered with pottery and other fragments of ancient life testifying to its former populousness: flint implements, among the rest. Of the interval between the latest of these stone-age primevals and the first Egyptian invasion of Gafsa we know nothing; they, the Egyptians, brought with them that plough which is figured in the hieroglyphics, and has not yet changed its shape. You may see the venerable instrument any day you like, being carried on a man's back to his work in the oasis.

Athwart this region there runs an underground (excavated) stream of water, led from Sidi Mansur to nourish the Gafsa plantations. Through holes in the ground one looks down upon the element flowing mysteriously below; figs and other trees are set in these hollows for the sake of the shade and moisture, and their crowns barely reach the level of the soil. This is no place to wander about at night—a false step in the darkness and a man would break his neck. There was talk, at one time, of leading this brook, which is sweet and non-mineral, into Gafsa for drinking purposes, but the native garden proprietors raised their inevitable howl of objections, and the project was abandoned.

If you ask a local white man as to the misdeeds of his administration, be sure he will mention the affair of the railway station which was built too far from the town, and this of the Sidi Mansur water. And who, you ask, was to blame for these follies? Oh, the ***controlleur***, as usual; always the ***controlleur!*** It is no sinecure being an official of this kind in Tunisia, with precise Government instructions in one pocket, and in the other his countrymen's contrary lamentations and suggestions, often reasonable enough....

Loaded down with a choice selection of Sidi Mansur flints, which are singular as having a white patina, I returned to Gafsa in the late afternoon and entered my favourite Arab cafe. Here, at all events, if you do not mind a little native ***esprit de corps***, you will be able to thaw your frozen limbs; all the other rooms of Gafsa, public and private, are like ice-cellars. There are many of these coffeehouses in the town, and this is one of the least fashionable of them. Never a European darkens its door; seldom even a native soldier; it is not good enough for them; they go to finer resorts.

At its entrance there lie, conveniently arranged as seats, some old Roman blocks, overshadowed by a mulberry, now gaunt and bare. It must be delightful, in the spring-time, to sit under its shade and watch the street-life: the operations at the neighbouring dye-shop where gaudy cloths of blue and red are hanging out to dry, or, lower down, the movement at the wood-market—a large tract of "boulevard" encumbered with the impedimenta of nomadism. There is a ceaseless unloading of fuel here; bargains are struck about sheep and goats, the hapless quadruped, that refuses to accompany its new purchaser good-naturedly, being lifted up by the hind legs and made to walk in undignified fashion on the remaining two. Fires gleam brightly, each one surrounded by a knot of camels couched in the dust, their noses converging towards the flame, while old desert hags, bent double with a life of hardship, bustle about the cooking-pots. There are brawls, too—Arabs seizing each other by the throat, raising sticks and uttering wild imprecations....

But within that windowless chamber, all is peace. Eternal twilight reigns, and your eyes must become accustomed to the gloom ere you can perceive the cobwebby ceiling of palm-rafters, smoke-begrimed and upheld by two stone columns that glisten with the dirt of ages. Here is the hearth, overhung by a few ancient pots, where the server, his head enveloped in a greasy towel, officiates like some high priest at the altar. You may have milk, or the mixture known as coffee, or tea flavoured in Moroccan style with mint, or with cinnamon, or pepper. The water-vessels stew everlastingly upon a slow fire fed with the residue of pressed olives. Or, if too poor, you may take a drink of water out of the large clay tub that stands by the door. Often a beggar will step within for that purpose, and then the chubby serving-lad gives a scowl of displeasure and makes pretence to take away the cup; but the mendicant will not be gainsaid—water is the gift of Allah! And, if so please you, you may drink nothing at all, but simply converse with your neighbour, or sit still and dream away the days, the weeks, the year, sleeping by night upon the floor.

A few of the customers are playing at cards or sedately chatting; others begin to prepare their favourite smoke of hashish. A board is called for and the hashish-powder spread out upon it. The operator chops it into still finer particles by means of a semicircular blade, deftly blowing away the dust—this brings out its strength. He is in no hurry; it is a ceremony rather than a task. Slowly he separates the coarser from the finer grains, his fingers moving with loving deliberation over the smooth board. Then the cutting process is repeated once more, and yet again. Maybe he will now add a little of the Soufi stuff, to improve the taste.

At last all is ready, and small pipes are extracted from the folds of the burnous and filled with half a thimbleful of the precious mixture. Two or three whiffs, deeply inhaled, stream out at mouth and nostrils; then the pipe is swiftly passed on to a friend, who drains the last drop of smoke and knocks out the ashes. Not a word is spoken.

Hand him your pipe, if you are wise, and let him fill it for you. This ***kif***, they say, affects people differently; but I think that, as a general effect, you will discover a genial warmth stealing through your limbs, while the things of this world begin to reveal themselves in a more spiritual perspective.

I thought of the sunset this afternoon, as viewed from Sidi Mansur. They are fine, these moments of conflagration, of mineral incandescence, when the sober limestone rocks take on the tints of molten copper, their convulsed strata standing out like the ribs of some agonized Prometheus, while the plain, where every little stone casts an inordinate shadow behind it, clothes itself in demure shades of pearl. Fine, and all too brief. For even before the descending sun has touched the rim of the world the colours fade away; only overhead the play of blues and greens continues—freezing, at last, to pale indigo. Fine, but somewhat trite; a well-worn subject, these Oriental sunsets. Yet the man who can revel in such displays with a whole heart is to be envied of a talisman against many ills. I can conceive the subtlest and profoundest sage desiring nothing better than to retain, ever undiminished, a childlike capacity for these simple pleasures....

A spirit of immemorial eld pervades this tavern. Silently the shrouded figures come and go. They have lighted the lamp yonder, and it glimmers through the haze like some distant star.

And I remembered London at this sunset hour, a medley of tender grey-in-grey, save where a glory of many-coloured light hovers about some street-lantern, or where a carriage, splashing through the river of mud, leaves a momentary track of silver in its rear. There are the nights, of course, with their bustle and flare, but nights in a city are apt to grow wearisome; they fall into two or three categories, whose novelty soon wears off. How different from the starlit ones of the south, each with its peculiar moods and aspirations!

Yet the Thames—odd how one's *kif*-reveries always lead to running water—the Thames, I know, will atone for much. It is even more impressive at this season than in its summer clarity, and as I walk, in imagination, along that rolling flood flecked with patches of unwholesome iridescence and crossed by steamers and barges that steer in ghostly fashion about the dusky waters, I marvel that so few of our poets have responded to its beauty and signification. They find it easier, doubtless, to warble a spring song or two. The fierce pulsations of industry, the shiftings of gold that make and mar human happiness—these are themes reserved for the bard of the future who shall strike, bravely, a new chord, extracting from the sombre facts of city life a throbbing, many-tinted romance, even as out of that foul coal-tar some, who know the secret, craftily distil most delicate perfumes and colours exquisite. The bard of the future ... h'm! Will he ever appear? As an atavism, perhaps. Take away from modern poetry what appeals to primitive man—the jingle and pathetic fallacy—and the residue, if any, would be better expressed in prose.

My neighbour, a sensible person, has ceased to take interest in the proceedings. Perched upright at first, his head drooping within the folds of his cloak, he has slowly succumbed; he has kicked off his sandals, stretched himself out, and now slumbers. I, too, am beginning to feel weary, and no wonder....

Primitive man with those flints of his, that weigh me down at this moment. This stone-collecting, *par exemple!* I wonder what induced me to take up such a hobby. The German Professor, as usual. Ah, Mr. Koken, Mr. Koken—those light words of yours have borne a heavy fruit. I possess four hundred implements now, and they will double the weight of my luggage and ruin my starched shirts, especially those formidable "praechellean" skull-cleavers. And I know exactly what the customs officer at Marseilles will say, when he peeps into my bag:

" *Tiens, des cailloux! Monsieur est botaniste?*"

And then a crowd of people will assemble, to whom I must explain everything, with the result of being arrested for smuggling forbidden mining samples out of a colony and ending my days in some insanitary French prison.

Chapter VI
AMUSEMENTS BY THE WAY

Meanwhile, to satiate myself with Gafsa impressions, I linger by the margin of the pool that lies below the fortress. Hither the camels are driven to slake their thirst, arriving sometimes in such crowds as almost to fill up the place. Donkeys and horses are scoured by half-naked lads; in the clearer parts, a number of tattooed Bedouin girls are everlastingly washing their household stuffs. Only on rare occasions is the liquid undisturbed, and then it shines with the steely-blue transparency of those diamonds that are a class by themselves, superior to "first-water" stones. At the slightest agitation all the accumulated ooze and filth of generations—rags and decomposing frogs and things unmentionable—rise to the surface in turbid clouds. The element wells out hot, from under the neighbouring Kasbah, with a pestiferous mineral aroma.

Hither comes, at fixed intervals, my friend Silenus, the water-carrier, on his philosophic donkey; nearly all Gafsa draws its supply of cooking and drinking water from this fetid and malodorous mere.

A fine example of French inefficiency, this "abreuvoir." Two hundred francs would suffice to tap the liquid a few yards higher up, by means of a common cast-iron pipe, whence it would rush out, pure and undefiled, to fill in a few moments those multitudinous water-skins that are now laboriously furnished, by hand, out of the often tainted pool below.

And of native inefficiency, likewise. Day after day, age after age, have these women done their laundry-work at this spot, and yet their clothing, for purposes of the work, is more hopelessly inadequate than the burnous of the males. They will arrive wrapped up in twenty rags that are always falling off their backs and shoulders (they possess no baskets). One by one these articles are removed, soaped with one little hand, stamped upon by two little feet, and laid aside. Nothing remains, at last, but a single covering garment—a loose chemise full of artistic possibilities for the onlookers. It gives the poor girls endless trouble, for it is continually slipping off their bodies on one side or the other, and one hand is engaged, all the time, in counteracting these mischievous movements. Standing as they do up to their knees in the water, it is tucked up high and of course tumbles down again every minute. At the end of their washing they are as wet as drenched poodles.

No harm in this, in summer-time; but with the thermometer below freezing-point they would suffer considerably were they not inured, like to other creatures of the desert, to every kind of discomfort.

The chief mental exercise of the Arab, they say, consists in thinking how to reduce his work to a minimum. Now this being precisely my own ideal of life, and a most rational one, I would prefer to put it thus: that of many kinds of simplification they practise only one— ***omission***, which does not always pay. They are imaginative, but incredibly uninventive. How different from the wily Hindu or Chinaman, with his almost preternatural sagacity in small practical matters! Scorn of theories is one of their chief race-characteristics, and that is why they end in becoming stoics—stoics, that is, as the beasts are, who suffer without knowing why.

There was one of these girls in particular whom I noticed every day, and whom, at last, I compassionately supplied with a couple of safety-pins, after explaining their uses. She was decidedly ugly. But sometimes you may see others here, with neatly chiselled limbs and elfish eyes of a sultry, troubling charm into which, if sentimentally disposed, you can read an ocean of love; these need not be supplied with safety-pins. An enthusiastic Frenchman at Gabes actually married one of these sphynx-like creatures—a hazardous and quixotic experiment. As brides for a lifetime (slaves) they cost from a hundred to six hundred francs apiece, and even more; and you will do well to ***abonner*** yourself with the family beforehand, in order to be sure of obtaining a sound article, as with the Tartar girls in Russian Asia and elsewhere. As a general rule, those of the semi-nomads—the Gourbi people—cost more than those of the true wanderers. The price varies according to the season and a thousand other contingencies; it rises, inevitably, in the neighbourhood of settled places, where employment of one kind (olive-picking, etc.) or another—chiefly of another—can be found for them.

One of the prettiest I ever saw was offered me for three hundred francs. It was an uncommon bargain, due to a drought and certain family mishaps. These little wildlings are troublesome to carry about. They are less nimble and amiable than the boys, and often require more beating than a European has time to give them. You can always sell them again, of course; and sometimes (into the towns) at a good profit.

The Arab woman is the repository of all the accumulated nonsense of the race, and her influence upon the young brood is retrogressive and malign. It matters little what happens in the desert where men and women are necessarily animals, but it does among the middle and upper native classes of the larger places. Here the French have established their so-called Arab-French schools, excellent institutions which are largely attended, and would produce far better results but for the halo of sanctity with which boys in every country—but particularly in half-civilized ones—are apt to invest the most flagrantly empty-headed of mothers. In Tunisia, as soon as the youngsters return home, these women quickly undo all the good work, by teaching them that what they have learnt at school is dangerous untruth, and that the Koran and native mode of life are the only sources of happiness. Then, to keep the son at home, the mother will hasten to catch a bride for him who shall be, if possible, more incompetent than herself, in order that she, the mother, may retain her ascendency over him. The father, meanwhile, shrugs his shoulders: ***Mektoub***! There is no fighting against such heroic perseverance on a woman's part; besides, was he not brought up on the same lines?

The mischief is done, for Arabs relapse easily; even native officers, who have served for years in the French army, will, on returning home, don the burnous, sit at street corners, and become more ***arabized*** than ever. So it comes about that, if the eyes of the former generation were entirely averse from French rule, the present one is Janus-faced—looking both ways. Some day, presumably, there will be a further adaptation, and their eyes, like those of certain flat-fish, will wander round and settle down definitely on the right side....

This is a favourite month for native weddings. There was one going on last night. I looked into the courtyard of a ruinous building which was crammed with spectators. The Aissouyiahs were performing, in honour of the occasion.

These are the dervish fanatics whom everyone knows. They eat scorpions, glass, nails, and burning coals; they cut themselves with knives and other instruments—impostors, for the most part.

It is mere child's play to what you can see further East.

Yet, with the starry night overhead, and the flare of torches lighting up a seething mass of faces below, of bronzed limbs and bright-tinted rags dangling at every altitude from the palm rafters and decayed stairway, the scene was more weirdly fascinating than as one generally sees it—in mosques or in the open daylight. There were wild strains of music and song; a wave of disquietude, clearly, was passing over the beholders. These performances, at such a time, may originally have taken place for purposes of nuptial excitement or stimulation; but it requires rather an exotic mentality to be stimulated, otherwise than unpleasantly, by the spectacle of little boys writhing on the ground in simulated agony with a long iron skewer thrust through their cheeks. They catch them young; and these scholars, or aspirants, are indubitably frauds and often worse than frauds. Mixed with them are a certain proportion of unbalanced, half-crazy individuals, who really work themselves into a frenzy and give the semblance of veracity to the entertainment. A judge of native physiognomy can generally tell the two types apart. There are also a few sensible men—butchers, porters, and the like—who do not mind a little pain for the sake of the profit.

For the rest, the ceaseless mandarin-like head-wagglings and mutterings of the names of Allah would stupefy anyone's brain up to a point. It is not only Arabs who daze their understandings with godly ejaculations, oft repeated. The marabout leader, who is a kind of ***maitre de ballet***, enfolds each performer in his arms and makes a few passes round him, or kisses him. The uninitiated then reel off in a trance of hypnotic joy; the others do the same, in more theatrical fashion. At the end of each one's trick he de-mesmerizes him once more, and perhaps touches the wound with his hands. He passes the skewer or sword between his lips as a disinfectant—a wise precaution.

These lacerations heal quickly. I have spoken to men labouring in the fields on the day following such excesses, and found them ready to "work" again the same evening.

It ended up with a beast-dance—two fine negroes, all but naked, depicting the amorous rages of panthers or some other cat-like feral. This was really good, of its kind; and if, as regards the earlier part of the programme, it was still difficult to tell where religion ended and sensuality began (it sometimes is), there was no doubt about the last item, which was purely sadistic. Soon there issued the familiar trillings from the balcony, and the firing-off of guns, to announce that the drama was terminated.

It is we shrinkingly aesthetic creatures who conjure up by a mere effort of the imagination what these blunt folks cannot conceive without gross visual stimulants. That is because they have not enjoyed our advantages; they are not civilized. Among other things, they have not gone through a "reformation." Take a northern stock, sound in mind and body; infuse into it a perverse disrespect for the human frame and other anti-rational whimsies; muddle the whole, once more, by a condiment of Hellenistic renaissance and add, as crowning flavour, puritan "conscience" and "sinfulness"—mix up, in a general way, good nourishment with ascetic principles—and you will attain to a capacity of luxuriance in certain matters that may well be the envy and despair of poor primitives like the Arabs.

Extremes meet. Performances such as these are beyond good and evil. They are for the wholly savage or the wholly civilized. We complain considerably just now of the swamping of class distinctions in our lands, but a man of culture has a prerogative to which the biliously moral middle classes can never aspire: to be an Arab, when it suits him.

Chapter VII
AT THE CAFE

Whether it be due to the incessant cold and dry winds, that parch the more genial humours, or to some other cause, there is certainly a tone of exacerbation, at this moment, among the European residents at Gafsa. I noticed it very clearly yesterday evening in the little French cafe—a soul-withering resort, furnished with a few cast-iron tables and uncomfortable chairs that repose on a flooring of chill cement tiles—where, in sheer desperation, two or three of us, muffled up to our ears, congregate before dinner to exchange gossip and imbibe the pre-prandial absinthe.

I announced my intention of leaving shortly for Tozeur.

"So you have not yet taken your fill of dirt and discomfort in Tunisia, Monsieur?" asked one of the clients. He is a wizened old nondescript with satyr-like beard, a kind of Thersites, who is understood to have established, from the days of Abdelkader and "for certain reasons," his headquarters at Gafsa, where he sips absinthes past all computation, exercising his wit upon everybody and everything with a fluent and rather diverting pessimism. "You will probably perish on the road to Tozeur, in a sandstorm."

"Ah, those sandstorms: they interest me. Have you ever been to Tozeur?"

"God forbid! Gafsa is quite bad enough for me. Or you may be strangled by the Arabs; such things occur every day. You smile? Read the papers! At some places, like Sfax, there are regular organized bands of assassins, the police being doubtless in their pay. Be sure to hold your revolver in readiness—better carry it in your jacket pocket, like this.... No revolver! (To the company at large) **He has no revolver**! In that case, don't dream of going out after sunset, here or anywhere else in this country. And read the papers."

It was always "read the papers."

I mentioned that I had walked home, at midnight on the previous evening, from the station.

"Then don't do it again, if you value your life. Not long ago a lieutenant was attacked on that very road, and almost beaten to death. He managed to crawl back to barracks, and is now a wreck, incapacitated from further service. By a miracle he was able to identify one of his assailants. They gave him—what do you think?—two years' imprisonment! Why not the **Legion d'Honneur** while we are about it? Then there was the Italian—a respectable Italian, for a wonder—who went out for a walk and was never heard of again. The country was scoured for two months, but not so much as a button was ever found—not a button! They had buried his body in the sand. That's their usual system, cheap and effective. And the guide-books say that Tunisia is as safe as the heart of France—ha, ha, ha! I wonder how much they are paid for making that statement, and who pays it?"

"The hotel proprietors, with an occasional subsidy from the Government." This from a bloodthirsty young extremist in gaiters and riding-breeches, who had once been a *colon*, a farmer, but had given it up in disgust. "We cherish these savages," he went on, "as if they were our uncles and aunts; everywhere, that is, save in those districts which are still under military rule. There you should see the natives stand up and salute you! I am anti-military myself; but I maintain that this salute should be kept up, as demonstrating the gulf that exists between ourselves and them. But the moment you leave that zone the gulf is systematically bridged over, to make it more pleasant for the poor, misused Arab. Let me tell you what I think. I think that the Sicilians would have managed things better than we have done. And I also think that our *controlleurs*, they are not Frenchmen, but Arabs."

"*Voyons, voyons!*" said a clear voice from another table—a new-comer, apparently. "These are the criticisms to which we are exposed, because we introduce an enlightened and progressive policy."

"Progressive policy be damned! We have held Gafsa for the last thirty years, and what have we done to improve the place? Nothing."

"Pardon me! We have planted twenty-seven pepper trees. Tunisia exists for needy people in search of work. If you can't make it pay, leave it alone. You have every facility for buying land, for importing this and that—why don't you settle down and make yourselves at home? A colony, my friend, is not an orchid."

"And as for those Sicilians," interposed the faun-like wooer of the Green Fairy, "I think you're all wrong. I admit that they are more flexible than we are, if you like to put it that way. They will do things that no Frenchman can do; they will establish themselves in places where no Frenchman could live; they will eat things which no Frenchman could swallow; they will oust the very Arabs out of the country in course of time, by sheer number of progeny and animal vitality. Oh, yes; it's clear the Sicilians can lower their standard to any extent. But they can never raise it. They are the cancer of Tunisia. Wherever they go, they bring their filth, their **mafia**, roguery and corruption. Every Sicilian is a potential Arab, the difference between them being merely external; the true African variety wears less clothes and keeps his house cleaner. I know them! A race of sinister buffoons and cut-throats, incapable of any ennobling thought, whose highest virtues are other men's vices, whose only method of reasoning is the knife.... Don't accuse me, Messieurs, of prejudice, when I am trying to state the case impartially."

You will often hear it put as baldly as that. The alien inhabitants of Tunisia are well hated by a certain type of Frenchmen. The country has been compared to a wine-bottle that bears some high-flown label indicative of fine stuff within—the French administration—but is filled, unfortunately, with a poisonous mixture from round the corner, the Jews, Sicilians, Maltese, and Corsicans.

It is as difficult for a tourist to arrive at a just opinion on this subject as for the average Frenchman. The traveller will not find it easy to acquire the necessary first-hand data, while the other is warped by his congenital xenophobia.

In 1900 there were 80,000 Italians, mostly Sicilians, in the Regency, as opposed to 20,000 Frenchmen, one-half of whom were Government servants. This great predominance of a foreign stock scared some good folks, and a "Comite du peuplement francais" was organized, to study ways and means of populating Tunisia with French citizens.

If Sicilians could obtain grants of land under the same conditions as Frenchmen, large tracts, now waste, would be converted into gardens, to the profit of the exchequer. Is it worth while? No, thinks the Government; and with reason. French rule in Northern Africa is a politico-moral experiment on a large scale, with what might be called an idealistic background, such as only a civilized nation can conceive. Italians might improve the land, but they could never improve the Arab; they are themselves not sufficiently wise, or even well-intentioned.

The Anti-Semitic agitation has died a natural death: you may curse the Jews, but you cannot crush them. They make good citizens, and are for ever trying to gain more political influence, which is surely to their credit, though it annoys a certain class in Tunis. As intermediaries between the Arab and the white man they are invaluable, their plasticity allowing them to ascend or descend in either direction, while their broad and active tolerance, fruit of bitter experience in the past, has honeycombed the land with freemasonry and scientific charity and liberalism. So far as I can see, their dirt does not detract from their astuteness—perhaps it aids it, by removing one source of mental preoccupation, cleanliness. The old distinction between Livornese and Tunisian Jews is slowly becoming effaced.

If there is one class of these immigrants whom the ordinary French employe hates more than another it is his own countrymen, the Corsicans. They have the gift of climbing into small but lucrative posts of administration, and there, once established, they sit fast like limpets, to the dismay of competing French office-seekers. Eject them? You might as well propose to uproot Atlas or Ararat. Not only can they never be displaced, but from year to year, by every art, good or evil, they consolidate their position. That done, they begin to send for their relations. One by one new Corsicans arrive from over the sea, each forming a centre in his turn, where he sits tight, with a pertinacious solidarity that borders on the superhuman.

Cave-hunting savages at heart, and enemy to every man save their own blood relations, the Corsicans are the nightmare of the Arabs on account of their irreclaimable avarice and brutality. They would flay the native alive, if they dared, and sell his skin for boot-leather. They can play at being ***plus arabes que les arabes***, and then, if the game goes against them, they invoke their rights of French citizenship in the grand manner. The Frenchman knows it all; he regrets that such creatures should be his own compatriots—regrets, maybe, that he is not possessed of the same primordial pushfulness and insensibility; and shrugs his shoulders in civilized despair.

As for the Maltese, they would be all very well if—if they were not British subjects. But such being the case, you never know! It is disheartening to find such babble in the mouth of respectable officials and writers.

I am well aware that there is a Sicilian *in fabula* who is not "mafioso"; that the crude banditism which sits in every Corsican's bones has raised him to the elysium of martyrs and heroes and not, where he ought to have gone, to the gallows; that the Maltese are not merely cantankerous and bigoted (Catholic) Arabs, but also sober, industrious, and economical. I have lived with all these races in their own countries and—apart from a fatal monkey-like apprehensibility which passes for intelligence but, as a matter of fact, precludes it—have found chiefly this to admire in them, that they are prolific and kind to their offspring.

Small praise? Not altogether. The same may apply to cats and dogs, but it does not always apply to civilized races of men. The Scotchman, for instance, can produce children, but is often unkind to them (**Read the papers!**); the Frenchman is kind to children, but often cannot produce them. It would seem that chiefly in half-cultured people are these two qualities, twin roots of racial and domestic virtues, to be met with side by side.

Whatever may be the cause of it—better food, a different legislation or climate, or contact with other nations—the suggestive fact remains, that the more objectionable idiosyncrasies of the Maltese, Corsicans and Sicilians become diluted on African soil. Can it be the mere change from an island to a continent? There may be some truth in Bourget's "oppression des iles." **Insulani semper mali**, says an old Latin proverb....

"Do you know," the gaitered young ex-farmer was saying—"do you know how many French **colons** there are in the whole regency? Eight or nine hundred, drowned in an ocean of Arabs, who own the land. And that's what we call settling a country. The Americans knew better when they cleared out the redskins! And how do the English manage in India? Why, they shoot them—*piff-paff*: it's done! That's the way to colonize (looking approvingly at me)—*supprimez l'indigene*! A nation cannot condescend to the idealistic ravings of an individual."

I observed that I had never heard of that method being actually adopted in India.

"You say that, Monsieur, because you fear it sounds a little drastic. But we are not in Paris or London just now; we can say what we think. Or better still" (glowing with enthusiasm), "they tie them to the mouth of a big gun, and then—**Boum ...**

houpla!! Biftek a la tartare."

"You are misinformed, my friend," said the voice from the other table. "That Indian cannon business was merely an administrative experiment."

I looked at the speaker, who was smiling mirthfully to himself. He was a fair-complexioned man of about forty-five, rather carefully dressed, blue-eyed, with a short, well-groomed beard—evidently an old acquaintance of the company.

"It's all right for you," the other retorted, "with your comfortable offices and your fat, ever-increasing salaries. You are not a harassed agriculturist, skulking in fear of his life, or a public servant, starving on four francs a day. Behold!" he went on, extracting a newspaper out of his pocket, "behold the latest portrait of yourself and your colleagues—you have an air of revolting prosperity. And your whole biography, too, in black and white; your wife, your children, your past career ... what it is to be a capitalist!"

"*Tiens*! I never saw this. And printed in Paris a fortnight ago! But it may be lying somewhere about the house. I only returned at midday, you know. Not exactly a flattering likeness...."

The document was handed round. It was a French journal devoted to mining interests, and contained a long article dealing with the phosphate industry of Metlaoui, near Gafsa, with views of the works and portraits of its principal representatives. Beneath that of the speaker were printed the words—

"PAUL DUFRESNOY,   Ingenieur civil des mines,"

and some other titles.

An odd coincidence, this meeting, on the eve of my departure.

I passed over to his table and mentioned that I possessed an introductory letter to him.

"How? And you are leaving to-morrow for the Djerid? You are not coming to see me?"

I replied that I would gladly give myself that pleasure. His family, he explained, was away just now, but if I could arrange to delay my departure for a little while he would accompany me as far as Metlaoui, which lies on the Tozeur route, and show me over the mines. He was to return to his work there in a week or so. The proposal was too tempting to be refused.

We spoke of the spirit of irritation and discontent that seemed rife among the

Europeans in Gafsa.

"Yes, the wind," he said; "or perhaps Africa generally. I've often noticed that men, and women too, put on new faces and characters hereabouts. This contact with an inferior race upsets their nervous equilibrium. The lack of comfort and the need of abrupt action makes them discard gentleness and other external husks of civilization. The mildest of us are liable to become brusque; and harsh ones, brutal. Only the native remains resigned."

Thereupon I propounded my hypothesis of the **Mektoub** or resignation doctrine: the intellectual burnous of the Arabs.

The theory, he thought, was so good that there must be something wrong with it. His work brought him into daily contact with the natives, and, so far as he could judge, **Mektoub** was only one aspect of their general way of looking at things. It was bound up, for instance, with that idea of impenitence. Unlike ourselves, who approve of self-abasement, the Arab regards repentance as only fit for slaves. He does not hunt for his own sins; he hunts for yours, and hits you on the head when he finds them. There was something in the notion, he thought, for surely remorse was rather a provincial sensation; it implies that a man has really done something wrong, or that he thinks he has; in either case, what was there to boast of? He had little time for studies, nowadays, but it seemed to him that the trend of feeling was in the direction of Old Testamentary ideals. Men were growing tired of offering their other cheek to be smitten; they found it degrading, as do the Arabs. Why not import some of these sterner conceptions into our morality, as we import their peppery curries and kouskous and pilaffs into our cuisine?

He was inclined to say amiable things about the English race. The Anglo-Saxon, he thought, with his "constitutional non-morality," had come nearest to discovering a sensible working system of conduct—as a nation. It is his highest racial virtue to lead the Cosmic Life—to take all he can get, and ask for more. That is why every one, in his heart of hearts, envies and admires him. His chief defect, he thought, was a disdain of a knowledge of general principles, justifiable enough in the times of unsound teleological theorizings, but not nowadays, when we have at last set foot upon earth.

"And what do you say," I asked, "to our so-called national hypocrisy?"

"Well, we others are apt to stand aside and marvel whether you have succeeded by reason of it, or in spite of it. Of course it annoys us beyond words! But there is a form of it which is highly laudable: the Anglo-Saxon, it seems to me, often acts in apparently hypocritical fashion out of consideration for what he conceives to be the opinions of the majority. Profoundly self-respecting, he is equally careful not to impinge upon the feelings of others, however wrong-headed he may think them. In such cases, his hypocrisy is only a proof of civilization and genuine politeness. Hence also that shyness and reserve which I have often noticed in your countrymen—they are not signs of awkwardness or indecision, but of strength systematically controlled."

"That is very gratifying. And what of our snobbishness?"

"The English snobbishness," he replied, "may not be beautiful, but its origins are sufficiently venerable to inspire respect. It testifies to long political stability; it is rooted in Magna Charta. We foreigners, who upset our Governments and annihilate our aristocracies every ten years, will never attain that mellow stage. One may dislike it; one dislikes the by-products of many excellent institutions. Your Government, for example, does extraordinarily little to foster art or literature or research. Taken by itself, that is an evil. But as a by-product of the English cult of the individual—of that avoidance of pestilential State interference in everything which is the curse of continental Europe—it may be gladly endured, if not admired."

He added:

"When one lives out of Europe, Monsieur, one learns to know England better. To see things at their true perspective one must take up a stand at a proper distance from them. England only begins to show its true proportions at a point where other lands cease to be visible. Austria, for instance, can only be examined on the spot. Once you have crossed the insignificant Mediterranean, this immense and fertile country, with its long history of rulers and battles, has already faded into air. ***Ca n'existe plus***. Your Gladstone explained the phenomenon correctly: Austria has never done good to the world."

I gathered that the Metlaoui phosphate company had modelled its principles on those of the "Anglo-Saxon." There is little "pestilential State interference" in its management; the board of directors takes all it can get, and asks for more. It is a paying concern, and consequently the shareholders admire it unreservedly—in the rest of mankind, this feeling is tinctured with a strong dose of envy.

Chapter VIII
POST-PRANDIAL MEDITATIONS

One dines early in Gafsa, and afterwards there is nothing, absolutely nothing, to do. Cafes become tedious with their card-games, cowboy politics and persistent allusions to "la femme," that protean fetich which dominates and saturates the Gallic mind, oozing out, so to speak, at every pore of their social and national life. They never seem to grow out of the *Ewig-weibliche* stage. If only, like the Maltese, they would talk less and do more in certain respects, the "comite du peuplement" might close its doors. But such recklessness would ill comport with the ant-like hiving quality which paid back, within I forget how few years, the German war indemnity.

After dinner, therefore, a short promenade about the streets and oasis, to court that illusive phantom, sleep, and to replenish the mind with new and peaceful images. I found a cloudless and relatively warm night. The wind had died down, and there was a brilliant comet (the Johannesburg comet) in the sky. Knots of natives were gazing at it with disfavour: I listened, and heard one of them attributing the Franco-Tripolitan frontier incident to its baleful fires. "And there is more to come," he added, "unless it goes away." Townspeople, of course; the cultivators are asleep long ago.

Why don't you settle down and make yourselves at home? With those words Dufresnoy had put his finger on the spot. The same idea must occur to every one who compares the French method of colonization with that pursued in English dependencies. Even our most ephemeral civil servants take pleasure in "settling down"; they acquire local interests in golf, or native folklore, or butterflies; they manage to surround themselves with an atmosphere of home. Among the **colons** of Tunisia you may find a home establishment of the most comfortable type, but Government employes regard the Regency in the light of an exile; they never try to make their life more endurable, as they easily could do, with a little co-operation.

In Gafsa, for example, where the summer temperature is 100, no ice can be procured unless you drive to fetch it from the station settlement where the phosphate company has its servants; if you want good vegetables, you must telegraph *inland* for them to Metlaoui, whither they are brought from the sea-coast, via Gafsa, for the consumption of the "company"; fresh fish, which are caught in fabulous quantities at Sfax, and could be transported by every over-night train, are hardly ever visible in the Gafsa market. There is no chemist's shop in the place, not even the humblest drug-store, where you can procure a pennyworth of boric acid or court-plaster. So they live on, indulging all the time in a luxury of lamentation.

There would be better shops in places like Gafsa if foreign commercial settlers were not discouraged from establishing themselves. French ones, needless to say, refuse to "settle."

The hotels in the country places, too, would be better. At present they exist on a system of monopolism and favouritism; it is quite beyond the ambitions of their managers to collect a clientele; most of these concerns are palpably run on the following principle: to keep the guest in such a state of chattering starvation, that he is *ready to eat anything*. How often have I yearned, in these "Grand Hotels"—they are all *grand hotels*—for the material comforts and the decent fare of some little wayside hostelry in Finland, or a rest-house in the jungle of Ceylon!

Why do French travellers not complain oftener?

Well, the Frenchman is a patriotic creature and congenitally kind-hearted; the proprietors of these establishments are country-people of his; they are poor devils who have got stranded, somehow or other, in Tunisia; one must have patience with them. Sometimes, however, your self-respecting Gaul is strained beyond the point of patriotic endurance by the concoctions of these Locustas and Borgias; then he unsheathes that dagger-like Neanderthal manner which he carries about with him for rare occasions of self-defence; and it warms the cockles of one's heart to hear how pertinently he discourses damnation to the cringing host. For we non-Frenchmen, be it understood, are all "des desequilibres" who demand toast, hot water and such-like exotics; our complaints need not be taken seriously; besides, foreigners are bound to pay in any case. But when a countryman begins to find fault there is not only a possibility that something, after all, may not be quite right with the cuisine or drainage, but even a chance that one or two items will be coldly struck off the reckoning. And that hurts!

They will tell you that there is nothing to be procured in the market; but if you proceed to the spot, you will at least see succulent legs of mutton exposed for sale. The **chef** of the establishment, however, when making his morning purchases, passes by these with scorn, and betakes himself to a little booth whose table is strewn with dubious scraps of skin and bones, which have already been fingered and contemptuously thrown aside by fifty dirty Arabs (I speak as an eye-witness); he buys a few handfuls of these horrors for three or four sous, and forthwith—hey, presto!—they are transformed into a "ragout a la bretonne" for the famished traveller. Tunisia is a sheep-rearing country—there are sixty thousand sheep in the **controle** of Gafsa alone—but you may live there a lifetime before seeing a leg of mutton at a country table d'hote. For all the "gigots" that ever appear at my host's entertainment, one might really think that the muttons of Africa were a peculiar species, a species without legs: crawling, maybe, on their bellies, like Nebuchadnezzar.

"Je m'en f—de vot' bon-homme," said one of these gentlemen to me, referring to Baedeker, with whose sacred pages I had threatened him. "And as for the tourists, they'll come just the same."

And so they do! But they all end in discovering that even the worm will turn, when suffering from the torments of **dyspepsia tunesina veridica sine qua non** ...

A good deal of amateurish talking is done, in Gafsa, in regard to the profits that would be gained were the oasis to be given over to Sicilian cultivators. Apart from the fact that the wealthy Kaid of Gafsa, who is the chief owner of it, would have something to say on the subject, these advantages would be limited to pruning the trees and grafting some of them; introducing, possibly, a few more vegetables, and having the ground more parsimoniously tended than at present. The magnesia in the water is hostile to the majority of delicate European growths. Something, no doubt, could be done in the way of improvement, but as a set-off to a visionary project of this kind, which is averse to the whole spirit of French rule in Tunisia, there would be a great rise in prices: Italians would form their inevitable ring. The extent of the gardens has almost doubled since 1880, without their help.

As to the Arabs——

If the French looked to their prison system they would soon arrive at better results. For childish thefts and such-like trespasses, committed nearly always at the instigation of their parents, boys of ten and twelve are now locked up with hardened criminals, often for considerable periods: what is this but a State-aided manufacture of crime? Go to the prison of Sfax, and you will realize that there may be some reason for the absinthe-drinker's remark as to the "organized bands of assassins" at that place. I speak of what I have seen with my eyes. I found the prison of Souk-el-Arba, for instance, so tightly packed with men and young boys that there was not room for all of them to lie down at night, and such furious fights used to occur for the possession of places near the wall (the room was in pitch-darkness) that the warder was obliged to enter, every now and then, and restore order by beating those nearest the door about the head with a club.

The Arab boy, they will tell you, is full of guile, and must be repressed.

Granted, but——

A colony, furthermore, is ***not an orchid***.

Granted.

Q.E.D.

Chapter IX
SOME OF OUR GUESTS

I shall be glad to leave for Metlaoui and the Djerid. Gafsa is losing its flavour; the novelty and pungency are gone. The same old faces, the same old ***bouts de conversation***; quickly, indeed, does one live oneself into a place and learn, or think to learn, all its little secrets.

The hotel, too, has suddenly become an insufferable menagerie. Mysterious inspectors come and go, and commercial travellers of unappetizing looks and habits are far more frequent than formerly. But I shall regret the earth-convulsing laughter of the Greek doctor, who has latterly taken to putting in an appearance at mealtime. He is a gruff, jovial personage, and so huge in bulk that he can barely squeeze into the door of his little shop in the ***souk*** where he sits, surrounded by unguents and embrocations, to treat the natives for their multifarious distempers. He is quite straightforward about the business. "You come to this country to spend money," he tells me, "but I—to make it."

The profession is not all plain sailing, however, for the French authorities raise every kind of obstacle in his path; they tear his red advertisements down from the street walls and openly call him a quack. Were it not for the Greek Consul in Tunis, who happens to be an old friend of his, who knows how much longer they would allow him to practise in the land!

I sometimes go to watch his operations, which, so far as I can judge, are fairly remunerative, thanks to Achmet the interpreter, one of whose many duties it is to inform himself confidentially of the financial status of prospective patients. For the richest sheikh will don tattered clothes when he visits the surgery, and would doubtless be taken for some poor labourer were it not for Achmet, who sees through the disguise and gives a discreet sign to AEsculapius, whose services, of course, must be prepaid; it is **_money down_** before he will prescribe or give away a drop of medicine.

I was much interested in one of his methods as exemplified on the person of a native youth who was led in the other day. He was an Aissouiyah dancer, and had evidently overdone his part in the heat of enthusiasm; there were no less than forty-three sword-cuts across his middle. After receiving a handsome fee the doctor gave him some liniment which caused exquisite pain: the patient writhed in agony.

"That's good medicine," I heard Achmet telling him, reassuringly; "that's strong. See how it hurts!"

For a while he bore up bravely, but the pain growing worse instead of better, the doctor was at last persuaded, out of compassion and in return for a second fee, to give him something with a more soothing effect.

But eye diseases are his speciality. His **_piece de resistance_** is a Jewish tradesman whom he has lately supplied with an admirable glass eye—a thing almost unheard-of in these parts. This man and myself were sitting in the shop not long ago when a Moroccan happened to be passing who had known him in his one-eyed days; the stranger gave him a sharp look and then walked swiftly away, apparently suspecting himself to be the victim of some absurd hallucination as regards the new eye. But he returned anon, to make sure of his mistake, I suppose; while the Jew confronted him with a defiant glance of his two eyes. They stared at each other for some time in silence. At last the Moroccan enquired:

"Are you the man who sold me that piece of cloth three weeks ago?"

"I am he."

There was another long pause. Then:

"That new eye: how came you by it?"

The Jew, a dreadful scoffer, pointed heavenwards with one finger.

"A thing of God!" he said. "A miracle has been vouchsafed me."

But the man of Mequinez answered nothing. He gazed at him once more, and then, slowly bending down his head, folded his hands across his breast in prayer, and walked away....

Then there is the Polish Count, Count Ponomareff, who arrived four days ago. He is past middle age, with a drooping moustache and large red nose; a wistful and woebegone figure, but a brilliant conversationalist, when the mood is upon him. I have not taken very kindly to the man. Among other things, he disapproves of flint-collecting; he asks, rather scornfully, "whether one can sell such stones." And yet, for some obscure reason, he has singled me out among the men as the object of his favourable notice, affecting rather a distant manner towards the rest of us; the ladies, however, are charmed by his courtly graces. He wears profuse jewellery, to set off his title, no doubt. It is understood that he has held high Government posts, and is now only waiting for some letters before joining certain friends in a costly caravan expedition further south. Yet he seems poor—hopelessly poor. I surprised him, soon after his arrival, in a heated debate with the landlord on the subject of candles and *cafe au lait*. Then he enquired if the country was safe.

"Not if you go out with a *machine comme ca*," touching the Count's gorgeous watch-chain.

He knows, at least, how to handle his knife and fork, which is more than can be said of all the inmates of this hostelry. A town-dweller, evidently; he tells me he detests wild life of every kind and has come here only to oblige his friends; he calls the Arabs "ignoble savages."

Such, however, is not the opinion of another guest, my friend Monsieur M——. One must be careful how one criticizes the habits of the natives in his presence; not that he would be angry, for he is too gentle to feel wrath; or become argumentative—he is too sure of his ground for that; but he might be wounded on his most sensitive spot, and he would certainly think you—well, misinformed.

The motley crew of Gafsa have become his favourites ever since his arrival in the country two weeks ago, and he has a theory that it is a mistake to endeavour to learn their language—it only leads you astray, it spoils the "direct impression."

He is a well-known French painter, whom some eye trouble has forced—only temporarily, let us hope—to abandon the brush. Despite his patriarchal beard, he is an impenitent romanticist of contagious youthfulness; the entire universe lies so harmoniously disposed and in such roseate tints before his mental vision, that no one save Madame M——, a wise lady of the formal-yet-opulent type, whom Maupassant would have classed as "encore desirable," is able to drag him to earth again, with a few words of wholesome cynicism.

Just for the fun of the thing, and to while away his hours of enforced idleness, he is collecting facts for a book to be entitled "Customs of the Arabs," as exemplified by the life of Gafsa. The idea came to him quite suddenly, after reading some descriptions which he considered sadly misleading. Customs of the Arabs! To tease him, I quote the authority of Bordereau, who says that there are practically no Arabs in Gafsa; that the customs of this town are one thing and those of the Arabs another, unless he applies the word Arab to all the Mohammedan races of these parts.

The objection is brushed aside; one word is as good as another, *n'est-ce-pas*?

I point out a genuine Arab who happens to be passing; he has come down from the hills and is leading a camel loaded with halfa; he is gaunt and ill-clad, but walks with a fine swagger, and is evidently a valuable young person, to judge by his tattooings.

"That? That's only a young savage from the mountains. How are you to find out anything about him? And I make a point, you know, of only recording what I see with my eyes. No theories for me! I mean to see everything and to set it down; to describe the Arabs as they are—as they *really are*, in all the circumstances of their daily lives. One must see everything."

As a painter, I urge, he must have discovered how useful it is to restrict the field of vision now and then; to be deliberately half blind.

"Painting, Monsieur, is one thing, and writing another. It is one of the few advantages of growing old that things begin to fall, so to speak, into their proper places. When I go to my studio, I go for distraction; art, it seems to me, is there to create moods, pleasurable or otherwise; a painter must seize impressions. But I go to my library for information; the business of a writer is to collect and arrange facts; a book, as I apprehend it, should be—a book. That is my quarrel with this Tunisian literature; many of the things that have been written about the country are not books at all; while others are full of mistakes. Look at these two volumes, for instance! Impressionistic realism, I suppose they would call it, scrawled down by an excitable female journalist who, I am sorry to say, has created quite a rage for European and American lady tourists among these Arabs, to the great discredit of our civilization. Read them, Monsieur, as a warning example, and perhaps you will give me your Bordereau instead; there may be something in it, after all."

I gladly make the exchange, and regard the transaction in the light of an omen, an epoch. I have been craving for something different from the facts of Bordereau, who has been my companion all these days. A solid little piece of work, by the way, which often set me wondering whether our British public would care to pay four shillings for a technical account of the climate, history and natural products of some remote Egyptian oasis. But perhaps the cost of production has been defrayed by some Government department.

These two volumes by Isabelle Eberhardt—where have I heard that name before?—look tempting. I promise myself some hours of pleasant reading.

"And then, for downright misstatement," he continued, "look at this. Here is a Monsieur Kocher, who passes for an authority, and who, describing the Arab marriage customs, talks of the 'brutalite du viol dans le marriage—un drame lugubre.' Now that comes of not examining things with one's own eyes. Since my arrival here I have already seen several Arab weddings and something of their married life, and I must say, candidly, that I find it full of romance. Say what you will, these Arabs are unconscious poets."

"And if you want still further information," I said, "ask the boy whom I saw blacking your boots this morning. He will describe to you the minutest details of his married life with surprising frankness. His father bought him a wife two weeks ago, under the condition, however, that his little brother is to be allowed to share in the joys of matrimony. That young savage from the mountains would blush, if Arabs ever could blush, to hear their revelations."

"Oh, oh, oh! You appal me! But I would like to make personal enquiries into the matter; that is, if I can make them understand me. It is my rule, you know."

"Do, Monsieur; question both the brothers, and write down their answers, the perusal of which will be a liberal education for our boys at home. Among other things, they say that whenever——But here is Madame coming!"

"Never mind her! She takes an interest in Arab institutions, as I do.... Only imagine, Amelie, our shoeblack is said to be actually married; and so is his little brother, and they have one and the same bride! Two husbands to one wife, or half a wife apiece—what do you think of that?"

"I think it's quite enough to begin with. Remember, **_mon cher_**, they are only children."

Chapter X
THE OASIS OF LEILA

I rode, for a farewell visit, to the small oasis of Leila, or Lalla, which lies a few miles beyond the railway station. It is one of several parasitic oases of Gafsa: a collection of mud-houses whose gardens are watered by a far-famed spring, the fountain of Leila.

The water gushes out, tepid and unpleasant to the taste—but health-giving, they say, like so many unpleasant things—from under steep banks of clay through which the railway to Sfax has been cut. It is a sleepy hollow of palms, a place to dream away one's cares. The picturesque but old-fashioned well at this spot has just been replaced by a modern trough of cement. I watched the work from beginning to end, ten or fifteen Arabs, supervised by a burly Sicilian mason, finishing the job in a few days.

"These Saracens!"—such was the overseer's constant lament—"these Saracens! You don't know, dear sir, what fools they are."

In never-ending procession of gaudy rags the village folk come to these waters, the boys mostly on horseback, the women afoot. Donkeys are loaded with the heavy black goat-skins of water; there is laundry-work going on, and a good deal of straightforward love-making under the shade. These children of nature have a wild beauty of their own, and the young girls are frolicsome as gazelles and far less timid. They have none of the pseudo-bashfulness of the townsfolk. For the rest, only the ***dessus du panier*** of womankind goes veiled hereabouts—a few portly dames of Gafsa, that is, who are none the worse, I suspect, for keeping their features hidden. Perhaps the good looks of these Leila people are a heritage from olden days, for this oasis is known to be a race islet, inhabited almost exclusively by men of the

Ellez stock—one of the three races that have chiefly contributed to the formation of the modern Gafsa type; a conquering brood of European origin, small but shapely.

But untold ages ere this the waters of Leila were already frequented by men of another kind, by the flint-artists. Among the relics of their occupation I picked up, here, an unusually fine implement of the "amygdaloid" shape.

Not a soul in Gafsa, native or foreign, could tell me who was the lady Leila that gave her name to this fountain. On the spot, however, I heard this tale: She was a young girl, madly enamoured of an Arab youth, but strictly guarded. Her married sister alone knew of their infatuation, and used to help her by keeping a look-out for him at the water-side; and when he appeared, she would return home and sing to herself (as if it were a snatch of some old ditty)—Leila, Leila, your lover comes! But the maiden understood, and swiftly, under pretence of fetching water, she would run to meet him at the well, and take her joy. The story has an air of probability; such things are done every day, at every fountain throughout the land. This lingering at the well is one of the moments when their hard life is irradiated by a gleam of romance.

An old man also gave me the following account:—

Ages ago, he said, when Gafsa belonged to the Sultan of Trablus (Tripoli) there was sad misgovernment in the land. The taxes became quite unendurable, and the city was half emptied of its inhabitants, who fled this way and that, rather than submit to the extortions of the Sultan's officers. And among those who escaped in this fashion was a god-fearing widow and her children. Her name was Leila. She took up her abode near this fountain, which was then little frequented. Here she dwelt, doing good works whenever occasion offered. And here, at length, she was received into the mercy of Allah and entombed. The country-folk gave her name to the water, to perpetuate the memory of her pious life....

The depression beyond this fountain is celebrated as the resort of game, and yesterday a French gentleman of my acquaintance went there, provided with all the accoutrements of sport, not omitting a copious luncheon-basket—there might be snipe or partridges, or perhaps a hare, a gazelle, a leopard—who knows?

He returned in good time for dinner.

"*Voila ma chasse*!" he said, opening his bag. It contained a bundle of wild asparagus, for salad, and fourteen frogs, which he had killed with a rifle.

"You can't get frogs as easily in my part of France," he told me. "If the sport were not forbidden for seven months out of the twelve, the species would long ago have become extinct."

I enquired whether the close-season for frogs was officially set down, like that of hares or wildfowl.

"Frogs," he explained, "are not considered game in the governmental sense of that word; they fall into the category of fisheries which, as you know, comes under the jurisdiction of the respective prefects. Hence the close-time, though officially fixed, varies according to the different provinces. In my department, for example, it begins on the 15th of January. At Gafsa, if I may judge by certain indications, it would probably be arranged to commence still earlier."

Far be it from me to decry the succulent hams of **Rana esculenta** (or rather *ridibunda*). I have been offered far more fearful wild-fowl nearer home—certain ornithological wrecks, I mean, that have been kept beyond the feather-adhering stage, and then reverently held before a fire, for two minutes, wrapped in a bag, lest the limbs should drop off.

There is considerable talk at Gafsa of the wild mountain sheep, the Barbary mouflon. They say that as late as the early nineties it was no uncommon thing to meet with flocks of over thirty grazing in the mountains. Although a special permit must now be obtained to be allowed to shoot them, their numbers have much diminished. But the accounts vary so wonderfully that one cannot form any idea of their frequency. Some talk of seventeen being shot in the course of two weeks' camping, others of three in a whole season. As a rule, they are not stalked, but driven, by an army of Arabs which the sheikh organizes for that purpose, towards certain openings in the hills where the sportsman takes up his stand. The desert lynx is sometimes met with, and hyenas, they say, occur as near to Gafsa as the Jebel Assalah. Arabs have told me that the fat of the hyena is used by native thieves and burglars to smear on their bodies when they go marauding. The dogs, they say, are so terrorized by the smell of it, so numbed with fear and loathing, that they have not the heart to bark. (Pliny records an ancient notion to the effect that dogs, on coming in contact with the hyena's shadow, lose their voice.)

Here, at the Jebel Assalah, I encountered a jackal—a common beast, but far oftener heard than seen. While resting in a sunny hollow of rock, I heard a wild cry which came from a shepherd who was driving the jackal away from his goats. The discomfited brute trotted in my direction, and only caught sight of me at a few yards' distance. I never saw a jackal more surprised in my life. When a camel expires in the plain near some nomads' tents, they sometimes set a spring-trap for jackals near the carcase—they eat these beasts and sell their skin for a few francs; the traps are craftily concealed underground, with a little brushwood thrown over them to aid the deception. It is impossible to be aware of their existence. But woe betide the wanderer who steps on them!

For the machine closes with the shock of an earthquake, a perfect volcano of dust and iron teeth leaping into the air. Its force is such that the jackal's leg is often cut clean off, and he hops away on the remaining three. For this and other reasons, therefore, it is advisable not to approach too near a dead camel.

The desert hare is shot or coursed with muzzled greyhounds, *sloughis*, who strike it down with their paws; unmuzzled, they rend it to pieces. There are few of them in Gafsa just now, on account of the cold to which they are sensitive; although muffled in woollen garments they shiver pitifully. Of falconers, I have only met one riding to the chase. It was the Kaid of Gafsa, a wealthy man of incalculable political influence both here and in Tunis. It is even whispered—But no; one must not repeat all one hears....

With the proprietor's permission I went over a young plantation of trees and vegetables that has sprung up near the railway line, about halfway between Gafsa and Leila. Excavating to a depth of six metres at the foot of the bare Rogib hill, they encountered an apparently unlimited supply of water, and here, where formerly nothing but a few scorched grasses and thorns could be seen, is now a luxuriant little oasis. More might be done with the place, but the owner seems to have lost interest in it; the locusts, too, have been rather destructive of late.

He had planted quantities of prickly pears, he said, but the Bedouins' cattle had devoured them. These are useful growths in Tunisia, requiring hardly any moisture and forming, when full-grown, impenetrable walls of spiky green. They also bring in a respectable revenue. In the district of Kairouan, for instance, many families draw their entire income from them. A few have been planted at Sidi Mansur and elsewhere near Gafsa, but they are unprotected and liable to be trodden down in their early years, or eaten. Barbed wire, herald of civilization, is almost unknown in these parts.

Like most tradespeople, this proprietor was rather despondent about the future of Gafsa. There had certainly been some improvement within the last twenty years—slight, but steady; the building of the railway station so far outside the town he considered a disgraceful piece of jobbery, a crime which had permanently injured the prospects of the place. Merchants, he said, are entirely dependent on the state of the Metlaoui mines. If, like last year, these do well, then Gafsa also thrives. If there is a strike or over-production, as at this moment, Gafsa suffers.

Tourists come to this town, he said, but they leave next day. Nothing is done to make their stay agreeable.

The natives are not of a kind to take much interest in its welfare. Gafsa has gone through too many vicissitudes to be anything but a witches' cauldron of mixed races. Seldom one sees a handsome or characteristic face. They have not the wild solemnity of the desert folk, nor yet the etiolated, gentle graces of the Tunisian citizen class; much less the lily-like personal beauty of the blond Algerian Berbers. Apart from some men that possess, almost undiluted, the features of the savage Neanderthal brood that lived here in prehistoric times, the only pure race-type that survives is one of unquestionably Egyptian origin, one to which Monsieur Bordereau, in his book on Gafsa, has already referred. No wonder; since Egyptian invasions of this region went on for centuries, culminating in the extended sea-dominion of Thotmes III at the end of the seventeenth century B.C.

A bastard Greco-Latin was the language of the place up to the thirteenth century A.D.

This confusion of blood has done one good thing for them—it has given them considerable tolerance in matters of religion. They are the least bigoted Orientals one could wish to meet. Only fifteen in a hundred, perhaps even less, perform the devotions prescribed by the Prophet. And it is part of their charming heterodoxy to be dog-eaters. They will catch and devour each other's dogs; they even breed them for the market, though they dare not expose the meat publicly, any more than that of swine, which they eat with relish. But up to a few days ago they had never ventured to touch the dog of a foreigner. On Wednesday evening, however, a fox-terrier belonging to a French official was found in the street, dead, with its throat cut. A stream of blood was traced from that spot to the door of a native eating-shop, and enquiries from the neighbours elicited the fact that the cook of the establishment had caught the beast and cut its throat; that the miserable creature, in its dying struggles, had escaped from his grasp and run in the direction of home, only to stagger by the roadside and expire from loss of blood.

There was a wild excitement over this little episode. The dog of a Frenchman killed, for culinary purposes, by an Arab; it was the ***comble*** of temerity! The owner of the animal, on hearing the news, buckled on his revolver and repaired to the shop with the avowed intention of shooting his man, whom the police, fortunately, had already conjured into some safe place of custody. If he is wise he will languish in prison for some days longer.

Gafsa lies high, and I ask myself whether its fierce shiftings of heat and cold, its nocturnal radiation that splits the very rocks and renders life impossible for many plants (outside the cultivated zone, which equalizes these extremes)—whether all this has not had a numbing and stupefying influence on the character of the inhabitants. Would not a man, under such perennial vexations, end in bowing his head and letting things take their course? I notice the climatic effect upon myself is a growing incapacity for mental effort. It is time to depart for the Djerid, where the sun, they say, still exhales a certain amount of warmth.

Add to this, Arab frugality and the cheapness of native living throughout the country, which removes all stimulus to work. A middle-class citizen tells me that he has just returned from Tunis, where a lawsuit had kept him for two years. He went there with an overland caravan which cost next to nothing; he slept in a ***zaouiah***, where he also obtained a bath gratis; he spent on his food four sous a day, neither more nor less, and by way of amusement took coffee with his friends or strolled down to the harbour to look at the ships. Six pounds in two years! And natives in authority, who are generally the richest, pay nothing whatever for their nourishment. Like the Kaid of Gafsa, they simply requisition it in the market; the sellers grumble, but conform to custom.

How quickly their looks can improve is shown by those who join the army. In a few months they grow fat, cheerful, and bright-complexioned, thanks to the hygienic life and better food. As it is, I have noticed single individuals among the poorest classes who look remarkably well as compared with their fellows. "They drink milk," was the explanation given me.

There is vitality enough among the young boys who play hockey—these ball games are non-Arabic, a relic of Berberism—and keep up the sport till late at night amid a good deal of ill-tempered fighting and pulling about. Their mothers' milk is still inside them; they have not yet succumbed to the ridiculous diet, clothing, and life-habits of their elders. But soon manhood descends upon them like a cataclysm; it tears them with a frenzy which is anything but divine and thereafter absorbs them, to the exclusion of every other interest. Hockey-sticks are thrown away....

That witchery of Orientalism, with its immemorial customs, its wondrous hues of earth and sky—it exists, chiefly, for the delectation of hyperborean dreamers. The desert life and those many-tinted, mouldering cities have their charms, but the misery at intermediate places like Gafsa (and there are hundreds of them) is too great, too irremediable to be otherwise than an eyesore. They have not solved the problem of the simple life, these shivering, blear-eyed folk. Their daily routine is the height of discomfort; they are always ailing in health, often from that disease of which they plaintively declare that "whoever has not had it, cannot enter the kingdom of Heaven," and which, unlike ourselves, they contract by their patriarchal habit of eating and drinking out of a common dish. They die like flies. Naturally enough; for it is not too much to say, of the poorer classes, that they eat dirt, and that only once a day. A fresh shirt in the year is their whole tailor's bill; two or three sous a day will feed them; sunshine, and the stone floor of a mosque or coffee-house by night, is all they ask for, and more than they sometimes get.

An old Arab song contains words to this effect: "Kafsa is miserable; its water is blood; its air is poison; you may live there a hundred years without making a friend." No doubt the plethoric Sicilian mason at the Leila fountain would thoroughly endorse this statement with his "Ah, signore—these Saracens!"... But one learns to like the people none the less. They are merely depressed; they are not deficient in mother-wit or kindliness; a little good food would work wonders.

The oasis people are milk-drinkers, and would be healthier than the townsmen but for the agues, fevers and troublesome "Gafsa boil" to which they are subject.

I go to these plantations at night-time, after dinner, when the moon plays wonderful tricks of light and shadow with the over-arching foliage. The smooth sandy stretches at the outskirts of the gardens shine like water at rest, on which the leaves of an occasional sparse tuft of palms are etched with crystalline hardness of delineation.

This untilled region is most artistic, the isolated clumps shooting up like bamboos out of the bare soil. The whole grove is still wrapped in its wintry sleep, and one can look through the naked branches of the fruit trees into its furthest reaches. Only the palm leaves overhead and the ground at one's feet are green; the middle spaces bleak and brown. But, do what he will, a man who has lived in the tropics becomes rather *blasé* in the matter of palms. Besides, there are no flints to be found here....

Yet such is the abundance of water that these Gafsa gardens have a character different from most African plantations. They are more artlessly furnished, with rough, park-like districts and a not unpleasing impression of riot and waste—waste in the midst of plenty.

Then there is a charming Theocritean bit of country—the temperate region at the tail-end of the grove. Only olives grow here; seventy-five thousand of them. Beside their silvery-grey trunks you may see herds of the small but brightly-tinted oxen reposing; the ground is pied with daisies and buttercups, oleanders border the streamlets, and the plaintive notes of the *djouak*, the pastoral reed of the nomads, resound from some hidden copse.

There will be nothing of this kind, I fear, in the carefully-tended oases of the Djerid.

Chapter XI
A HAVEN OF REFUGE

The cold being past all endurance and belief, I was tempted to fulfil my promise and call upon Monsieur Dufresnoy. What kind of man was this that managed to survive it?

They led me to his house, which is one of the few two-storied buildings of the town and lies in a squalid street of mud-dwellings. Villainously dirty walls surround a massive entrance-gate studded with nails and bands of iron, intervolved in artful designs. No bell, no knocker, no door-handle; only an impressive lock. At the sight of this doorway I paused—it was grim, claustral, almost menacing; there was an air of enchantment about the mansion, as if once in a hundred years its forbidding portals might turn on their rusty hinges.

Finally, I fled away altogether, in a kind of godly panic.

M. Dufresnoy, on his way homewards, almost ran into me. I tried to explain the sensations his domicile had aroused in my mind; he laughed at first, and then admitted that he had often felt the same thing. The house was apt to look like that, he said, when his wife was away.

The inside appearance, once that portal has been passed, is quite different, and I was glad to have an opportunity of seeing the place, as it is one of the surprises of Gafsa, one of the few remaining town-houses that date from better days, being built originally for some Turkish grandee or governor—for him, I daresay, who drove the god-fearing widow to the sylvan seclusion of Leila. You step through the gate into an open square patio, surrounded, on the sides not abutting on the street, by an arched passage that reposes on old Roman columns. This covered loggia, running round three fronts of the court, is the feature of the house: wonderful how a few arcades and pillars will impart an air of distinction and even luxury! Almost nothing has been done to change the old appearance of this small but well-proportioned patio; the walls have been freshly whitewashed, the original mud-flooring replaced by tiles, a bright flower-bed set in the centre—nothing more.

The five or six lower rooms to which the loggia gives access must be delightfully cool in summer, but they are dark and chilly at this season. Luckily, the mansion possesses an upper story where the family resides during the winter, in rooms that are actually floored with wood. From here, looking out of the windows, there is a wondrous view over a wilderness of decayed Arab dwellings upon the oasis beyond, and the distant purple mountains.

There is an irresistible air of geniality about this home: can it be the house itself? For a subtle influence, no doubt, penetrates to the heart of man from the mere form and disposition of inanimate things. I was prepared to be smothered in a profusion of local effects; of saddle-cloths, silk hangings, water-pipes, daggers and match-locks, dim nooks with divans, and those other decorations that suggest the glamour of the Orient to certain Western minds. Or again, I said to myself, this European wife will have imported certain tastes from over the sea; the house will be replete with trifles carefully disposed in negligent fashion, silver photograph frames and flower vases reposing on diminutive tables, and such-like indications of what our novelists call the "tender but indefinable touches of a woman's hand."

Nothing of the kind. The place is simply comfortable: it appeals to one's sense of propriety. There are carpets and genuine arm-chairs—unique phenomena in this part of the world; best of all, fire-places wherein ample logs of olive-wood glimmer and glister all day long.

And so the last few days have passed. Mentally, too, I am thawing once more; the hotel life and solitary walks of Gafsa had begun to affect me disagreeably. Such things are endurable and perhaps stimulating in youth and in the plenitude of health; but there comes a period when one lives less in future dreamings than in the experiences of the past—unpleasant company, for the most part; when one craves to see the faces and hear the opinions of rational fellow-creatures; when one requires, in short, to be distracted. This is the age, too, at which a man begins to realize the significance of those once-despised material comforts. Tunisian hotels can only be inhabited by young hopefuls.

The house contains a considerable library of local literature—mostly technical and dealing with Dufresnoy's Metlaoui district, but some of it intelligible to a simple traveller like myself. From certain books I have begun to make extracts concerning the places I am likely to visit: Metlaoui, the Djerid oases, and the Chott country.

Dufresnoy is essentially a mining engineer. He evidently knows his business thoroughly; he has been employed in various parts of the French dominions and likes the work; all of which has not prevented him from becoming a man of the world and keeping his other intellectual pores open. There is nothing of the professional in his conversation. He is rather undemonstrative, for a Frenchman.

He told me an odd thing about the native rising in Thala in 1896, when a marabout preached death to all foreigners, with the result that several white men were murdered (it was a hastily collected band of Italian tradesmen who put down the insurrection). They caught him, and in due time he died (?) in prison—they were probably afraid to execute him: perhaps he killed himself—and the odd thing is this: that although the necessary sum has been contributed for erecting a monument to these unhappy victims of native ferocity, yet the Franco-Tunisian authorities are averse to the plan, on the ground that such a public monument might offend Arab susceptibilities. This struck me as overdoing the "pacific penetration" policy; and he thought so too, more especially as there is a commemorative stone to some preposterous native bigot at the very place....

I shall be sorry to leave Dufresnoy at Metlaoui. In him I often admire that fine trait of his race: the clarifying instinct. He possesses—with no pretension at knowledge beyond his mining sphere—an innate rigour of judgment in every matter of the mind; he avoids crooked thinking by a process of ratiocination so swift and sure as to appear intuitive. Even as a true collector of antiques has quite a peculiar way of handling some rare snuff-box or Tanagra statuette and, though unacquainted with that particular branch of art, yet straightway classes it correctly as to its merits, so, to him, an idea of whatever kind is an ***objet de vertu***, to be appraised with unfailing accuracy. He is a connoisseur of abstractions. What the Goth carves out grotesquely after a painful labour of mental elimination, the right deposited, as residue, after a thousand wrongs—what the Latin smothers under a deluge of mere words: this your Frenchman of such a type will nimbly disentangle from all its unessentials; he presents it to your inspection in reasonable and convincing shape—purified, clipped, pruned. What is this gift, this distinguishing mark?

Discipline of the mind, culminating in intellectual chastity—in what may be called a horror of perverse or futile reasoning.

He mentioned, incidentally, the case of suicides among the natives to prove that the *Mektoub* doctrine is not wholly pernicious. Suicides were quite unusual, he said; the Arabs do not seem to be able to fall in with the idea, preferring to bear the greatest evils rather than take an active part in the undoing of themselves. That was *Mektoub*: to bow the head, dumbly resisting. And were they not right? Did not the great majority of European cases of suicide imply a neurotic condition—such as when men of business have suffered reverses on Exchange or lost some trivial appointment? How easily things could be bridged over, or repaired, or even endured! The most hopeless invalid could testify to the fact that some pleasure can still be extracted out of a maimed or crippled existence; a man, however impoverished, might still live in dignified and fairly cheerful fashion.

He thought that in the matter of suicides, as in that of remorse, we were too "spectacular and altruistic"; that we lived in a rather unwholesome atmosphere of self-created and foolish ideas concerning honour and duty; that the *Mektoub* practice of the Arabs pointed to an underlying primitive sanity which we would do well to foster within us.

Chapter XII
THE MYSTERIOUS COUNT

Gafsa, even Gafsa, has its enigmas.

I climbed this afternoon to the summit of the Rogib hill, which lies near the railway station, on the further side of the Oued Baiesh. This, presumably, is the site where Marius halted for the last time before attacking the town; and the spot was also interesting to me on account of its flint implements....

A sad and barren range of hills. There was no sunshine, for a scirocco-storm raised clouds of dust and obscured the sky; the wind was bitterly cold. Finding it impossible to attune my phantasy to the picture of Marius and his soldiers, I descended once more.

On the station turnpike I overtook a solitary foot-passenger, who plodded slowly along. It was the Polish Count. He had been absent from the hotel for several days, and now appeared to be in the gloomiest of humours.

Where had he been?

For a promenade, he said. It was too dreary sitting indoors, all alone. He had left the hotel. The place was too noisy: the dogs barked incessantly. He had taken rooms with a Jew, and arranged to have his meals at a small Italian *trattoria*.

This was a half-truth, I felt sure. The dogs of Gafsa, no doubt, are past all endurance; they are worse than in any Turkish village where they howl at least in unison, and so continuously through the night that one ceases to take note of them; but the man's real reason for this change of domicile was probably another one.

"You must find that much quieter," I said, "and cheaper as well. These hotels are rather pretentious."

"Pretentious and dear. Here I am, stranded in an unknown place, without friends; remittances are due to me, and they never come"—he broke into the subject without reserve—"and it is hard, I assure you, to deprive oneself of things, of trifles, if you like to call them so, to which one is nevertheless accustomed and entitled, so to speak, by birthright. But I am talking to the winds, no doubt. You, Monsieur, are one of the fortunate ones; you don't know—you don't know——"

"Yes I do," I replied, trying to think of something to say in the way of consolation. "I know quite well——"

"How do you know?" he interrupted. And next, with needless vehemence: "**What** do you know?"

I was surprised at his sudden change of tone. It was awkward, all this. I gave utterance to such commonplaces on the instability of human affairs as occurred to me, and ended up by offering, I hope with sufficient delicacy, to assist him to the small extent that lay in my power.

"Ah!"

He seemed infinitely relieved by my words: he evidently expected some answer of quite another import. Turning his back to the wind, and pausing for a moment to adjust his clothing, he replied, with ambassadorial deliberation:

"You may be certain, Monsieur, that I would not easily forget a kindness of this nature; my lot in life has been far too unhappy to make me undervalue what you, a stranger, have just offered me. But I will decline: what are a few francs to me? Pray don't think me ungrateful, however. You have caught me in an almost delirious moment, and your friendly words just now, when I felt myself so abandoned and in so critical a state of mind, with this dreadful desert wind moaning and everything, as it seems, hostile to me: your kind words, I say, touched me more deeply than I can express." (Here he wiped away a genuine tear.) "But my luck may yet turn, and then, be sure, I will make you forget all my childish querulousness."

And he went on, almost gaily:

"I never could keep money! And the worst of it is, I hate work; I was not brought up to it, and you will admit that I am too old to begin life anew. Yet I object on principle to so-called charity, being intelligent enough to know that there is only one kind of charity, and Justice is its name. But what is justice? I suppose we all possess some kind of natural rights, according to our stations; justice, I take it, would consist in our being permitted to enjoy those rights. If this is correct, then—ah, Monsieur, the demoralizing effects of poverty, of non-justice, on a man like myself; how it lowers your self-respect and makes you capable of actions that you would reprobate, in your right mind—"

"In your right mind? Is a poor man, then, insane?"

"How can I make you understand? Tell me, is not poverty a kind of madness, an obsession that haunts you night and day? To puzzle, at every hour, how to meet this demand and how to shun that one; to deny yourself the necessities of life, and your friends those poor little pleasures that you are yearning to bestow upon them—is it not a mental malady, a fever; is it not damnation itself? The thousand meannesses: how they degrade you; how they suck away your strength, your ambition, your faith! To see no openings before you, save ever darker gulfs of despair! I cannot hope to make you conceive such a hell: one must have been there oneself. But note this, Monsieur: never judge an impoverished man by your own standards of right and wrong—never! For the old-established meanings of things shift for him—they shift; and his temptations become formidably subtle beyond belief. When rich, he says calmly ***Non; ca ne va pas***. But to forego an advantage, when poor, is the same as if—let me see ... as if one asked you to leave lying some fascinating flint in the desert waste."

"That simile, surely, is all wrong, Count. Nobody can be injured by my flint-mania, whereas——"

"I know, I know; I am not trying to excuse things; I am only explaining how they happen. But how explain to others? We always talk of putting ourselves in our neighbours' place; idlest of phrases! since we cannot possibly avoid bringing our personal apparatus to bear on their problems. There is a gulf between man and man. You will hardly believe that I used to take an interest—quite superficial, you know, but none the less real—in all those questions of the day that absorb the ordinary man of ease, in politics and art and whatnot; but nowadays all my interests are centred on one single point. On what point, do you think? On keeping up the external appearance, and the manners, of well-being. I have no energy left for anything else; and even this effort quite exhausts me. Art and politics! What, in the name of heaven, do I care for art and politics, with the knife at my throat? I only utilize these things; yes, I utilize them for conversational purposes, in order to deceive others as to my true, incessant and miserable preoccupations. Laughable, is it not? Why don't you smile, Monsieur—you, who have never known the bitterness?"

We were crossing the broad Oued Baiesh, a stretch of yellow sand and stones. To obviate damage by sudden floods, the French have covered this tract of the road with a coating of asphalt; but the busy life here, the droves of camels and sheep, the Arab folk laughing over their laundry-work in the shallow streamlet that trickles through the waste—all these things were gone for the moment.

But for the torn line of Gafsa palms that confronted us on the other side of the river-bed, we might have been in the veriest wilderness. Although the wind was lulled, petulant little pillars of sand still arose here and there among the boulders, and sank down again, as if exhausted; the descending sun had emerged, a lurid disk, framed in a sulphureous halo that melted imperceptibly into the gold of the west.

It was growing chillier than ever, and the Count, shivering with cold, drew his burnous more closely about him; he had bought one for fifteen francs, probably in imitation of myself, or because I once jokingly called it "a garment for millionaires who need not use their hands." He liked to be taken for a millionaire.

I looked at him awhile, wondering what thoughts were ruling the expression of his perplexed and sorrowful features, and then tried to turn the conversation into other channels.

"Are there interesting people at your Italian restaurant?"

"Well, there is Hirsch, the young German: you know him?"

"The police commissaire was talking to me about his case yesterday."

"Ha, was he? Let me tell you that I have investigated it thoroughly, and find it most instructive. This young fellow is not yet twenty; he ran away from home for no discoverable reason, then signed on a merchant vessel at Marseilles and, disliking the work, slipped out as soon as she touched port at Sfax, and climbed without a ticket into a night-train, thinking to reach Tunis. Instead of that, he woke up in the morning and found himself at Gafsa! Here, you see, are all the elements of wrong-doing, and the authorities have learnt his history from his papers which they seized. As a German and a Jew, the French instinctively dislike him; as a Jew and a foreigner—the Arabs; he is objectionable to look at, dull of wit, and knows not a word of French or Arabic. But he is poor, and therefore—every one loads him with kindness."

"And why not?" I asked.

"Why not, indeed? Your friend the magistrate has given him some money out of his own pocket; the restaurant proprietress refuses to be paid for his food, while another one, near the station, sends word to say that he can have a plate of soup there whenever he likes; a young Arab boy—these Arabs are really incomprehensible—gives him as many cups of tea or coffee as he can drink; a Jewish lawyer has sent him some clothes; a gentleman in your hotel a quantity of linen; the Italian barber shaves him gratis; a certain shopkeeper sends him a bottle of liqueur—of liqueur!—every second day; the commissaire has given him, free of charge, a decent unoccupied bedroom in the prison, where he can go in and out as he pleases; best of all, the **Ponts et Chaussees** are now employing him at three francs a day—a princely income, they tell me—at some agricultural job: pure kindness, inasmuch as he has never handled a spade or pickaxe in his life. He can have a pleasant time in Gafsa; he can marry an heiress if so disposed; then, when the place begins to bore him, the German Consul in Tunis will repatriate him at his Government's expense. 'He's a poor devil,' they say. Why do I tell you all this? Because—well—I am also poor—"

Always harping on the old theme!

"The cases are not quite parallel, are they?"

"No. He is young, and fit for work, whereas I am past the middle term of life. Old age—another horror! Besides, I am a gentleman——"

"Exactly. We should be ashamed to shave you gratis."

"I suppose you're right, Monsieur. I was only trying to explain—to explain myself—to myself, I mean. Pardon me if I speak too much of my wretched affairs. But I'll tell you what I think. To endure this revolting destitution a man must be an Arab. Now, I cannot pretend to be an Arab; I would not adopt their ideals if I could. And yet, alas! I am beginning to believe in predestination, as they do; to believe that our faults and our virtues are distilled beforehand in the silent laboratory of the past. A sad creed, to think of men born to misfortune; to be obliged to consider yourself—how do you say in English?—*a stepchild of nature*...."

He was always a good talker, but it is impossible to describe the intensity of feeling in his speech to-day. He seemed to suffer from some imperious need of unburdening himself, even to a chance acquaintance like me; long days of loneliness, maybe, had worked on his nerves and produced a kind of congestion. But in his words and voice I detected lapses into other moods, into some other state of being; they gave me the impression as of two different individuals addressing me. The man did not ring true, altogether; he was mentally disorganized, disharmonious; those meretricious reasonings about justice, for example, struck me disagreeably.

And I could not help contrasting his rambling emotionalism with the logic—the relentless, diamond-like *justesse*—of the mining engineer. He is the very antithesis of that pellucid and homogeneous character. The sanguine temperament ...

What is a man of this type doing in Gafsa?

Mystery!

The rest of us, the cynical Greek doctor, the artist-sage and lover of Arab institutions, myself (flint-maniac)—to say nothing of men like Dufresnoy—we all contrive to fit, after a fashion, into the place; we have a *raison d'etre*. But this composite, unadaptive city-dweller: how incongruous a figure against that background of palms and barren mountains!

An enigmatical creature, and yet not wholly unlovable; he may be unsound or even unprincipled, he may be deficient in qualities that go to make men respected and satisfied with the world in general, but he possesses, I think, certain citizen-virtues unintelligible to the self-centred, rustic type of mind. He could be stirred to acts of unworldly enthusiasm; he would share his last crust with some shipwrecked sailor, or shed his blood gaily for a generous idea. And he is plainly in hard case just now.

A stepchild of nature....

"You have a very good English accent, Count."

"We were carefully brought up in languages. Not every one understands Polish, you know."

"By the way, how does it come about that you, being a Pole, should have a Russian family name?"

The question seemed to astonish and perplex him. At last he said:

"Oh, it's about the same thing, isn't it? Nowadays, I mean," he added, with grandiloquent pathos, "ever since the misfortunes of my unhappy country."

At the entrance to the town we separated, and I watched for some time his bowed form as it crept along the wood-market in the direction of the Kairouan road.

This is one of the figures that will persist in my mind very clear and pathetic, and I shall long remember those plaintive remarks about poverty that welled up, surely, from the bottom of his heart. How far, I wonder, is such a man the author of his own calamities, and how far have they **made him**? Academic questionings, based on out-of-date philosophy! Our vices, he said, are distilled for us beforehand in the dim laboratory of the past. His vice, evidently, is to hate work of every kind; his faculties, therefore, never undergo the rhythmic joy of reaction, for he is too well nourished to live the *vita minor* of a starveling, to endure Arab acquiescence in non-production.

"I am only trying to explain myself—to myself." Half-truth, I imagine. He is probably conscience-stricken, or at least dissatisfied with his conduct for one reason or another, and endeavouring to justify some base plan of action by re-stating ethics in terms of hunger; a specious line of argument, since hunger is not the rule but the exception.

And then I shall think of his red nose and watery little eyes, his absurd jewellery—a fine presence, none the less, when he pulls himself together; there is about him an air of faded distinction that softly symbolizes the history of his adopted country.

The Count!

Why a count? Because all Poles are counts—those that are not princes. But why a Pole? Well, perhaps from the convenience of vagueness, inasmuch as there is something international about a Pole—international, and yet neither equivocal nor vulgar; every one sympathizes with them, for they all possessed, once upon a time, vast estates whose loss is borne in cheerful resignation, and never so much as alluded to; they know everybody, and everybody worth knowing is related to them, by marriage or otherwise, in this or some other century; as men of the world, they are ready to talk upon any subject with tolerance, geniality and a pleasingly personal note that withers up the commonplace, smoking, meanwhile, innumerable cigarettes out of mouthpieces which display a complex escutcheon contrived in gold and rubies upon the amber surface. Yes, his choice was good: Poles are gentlemen. But why caricature them? And why, above all things, select an inappropriate Muscovite name? That argues a lack of general intelligence and might easily spoil everything; so true it is, as a legal friend once observed to me, that "it takes a wise man to handle a lie. A fool had better remain honest."

What can be the meaning of this unlovely comedy? Some defalcation or forgery? Likely enough. But I think he lacks the cleverness requisite for a habitual criminal. Perhaps he is only a poor survivor, drifting about in lonely and distracted fashion while waiting for the inevitable end. Others may solve the enigma, but not I; for to-morrow we go to Metlaoui.

Yet I know that long after the palms and minarets of Gafsa have faded into the blurred image of countless other palms and other minarets, I shall be able to call up the figure of this forlorn and ambiguous fellow-creature, standing on the asphalt of the river-crossing with his cheap burnous wrapped around him, sighing, shivering, and setting forth certain views concerning human life for which there is, after all, a good deal to be said.

Chapter XIII
TO METLAOUI

I should be sorry to say how long the train takes to crawl through the thirty odd kilometres that separate Gafsa from Metlaoui. My companion on the trip, M. Dufresnoy, tells me that the return journey is still slower, because the line runs mostly uphill and the trucks, thirty or forty of them, are loaded with minerals. Fortunately, the car in which we travelled—each train has only a single passenger carriage—was comfortable, being built after the fashion of the Swiss "Aussichtswagen," with seats on the exterior platform whence one can admire the view.

It gave me some idea of the goods traffic (phosphates) along this line when he told me that during the past seven days 23,000 tons of mineral had been conveyed to the port of Sfax alone, to say nothing of those that had gone further on, to Sousse and Tunis. And not long ago, he said, the company had an unpleasant surprise: sixteen new engines of a powerful type, which they had ordered from Winterthur, were suddenly discovered to be liable to a duty of 1000 francs apiece as "imported articles."

"We can afford it," he said. "Our five hundred-franc shares are standing at three thousand seven hundred francs."

But he thought that a grave error had been committed in selecting the narrow metre gauge; it was all very well for phosphate transport, but once the line over Feriana and the branch to Tozeur are completed, they would have to deal with other material, such as tourists, that require fast services.

They had an accident last year. The couplings of a train, climbing uphill from Gafsa past the Leila oasis, suddenly broke, with the result that the rear portion rushed backwards again, careered through the Gafsa station and up the artificial incline which leads towards the Oued Baiesh, crossed the bridge, and thundered at a vertiginous pace into the desert beyond. As luck would have it, another train was just then approaching Gafsa. They collided with terrific force and, telescoping being out of the question since both were loaded with minerals, escaladed each other in Eiffel-tower fashion. Arab eye-witnesses say that the stoker of the up-train was thrown out by the impact and flew across country "like a bird" for half a mile; he alighted on his feet, and was found, after a week or so, wandering about the plain in a dazed condition. The driver was killed outright, and his widow draws a respectable pension from the company.

Since then two engines are always employed to move the train up the few miles beyond Gafsa.

The cream-tinted level is speckled with white incrustations and sombre tufts of desert herbs; here and there, where the winter's rain lingers underground, are spots of brilliant green; short-lived crops of corn, sown by the nomads. The hills to the right of the line are bare and torn into wild ravines; lilac-hued patches, ever changing and fair to see, move among their warm complexities: cloud-shadows. Here, if anywhere, one learns that shadows are not always grey or black; even those cast in moonlight have a certain ghostly coloration.

It was a marvellously clear day, and not many miles before reaching our destination we looked back upon the downhill route traversed which, so far as one could see, might have been a dead level. At a distance of nearly twenty miles Gafsa was plainly visible—white buildings piercing a dusky line of palms—an hour's walk, it seemed. I observed in the brushwood a couple of bustards, their heads peering above the herbage. These birds are rather rare hereabouts, and shy of approach. Arabs say that the bustard is like the camel: once it begins to run, you never know when it will stop. They surround them therefore cautiously, and gradually close the circle to within shooting distance.

Metlaoui is the name of two distinct villages which have been conjured out of the waste by the discovery of its phosphate deposits—the station village and, a mile or so further on, Metlaoui proper, with its big establishments for working the minerals.

Here already, at the station settlement, there is more life than in Gafsa, though the surroundings are decidedly unpropitious—a waterless plain, with low hills in the foreground, phosphate-bearing, and wondrously tinted in rose and heliotrope. There are respectable stores here, very different from the shops of Gafsa. I entered a large Italian warehouse which contained an assortment of goods—clothing, jams, boots, writing-paper, sealing-wax, nails, agricultural implements, guns, bedding, mouse-traps, wire, seeds, tinned foods—and vainly endeavoured to think of some article which a *colon* might require and not find here. The only drawback is that there are no "colons" in the district.

While waiting for a conveyance to take me to the industrial settlement, I strolled about and found my way across a sad stretch of ground littered with tin cans, bottles, and other refuse, to a slight eminence whereon lay a cemetery. In this forlorn square are about twenty tombs, already crumbling to dust, although not one of those I saw was five years old. Humble victims for the most part—Italians in the prime of life who had come to these regions to gain a little money; or little children, carried off by the harsh climate (yet the climate of this place is preferred to that of Gafsa). The enclosure is filling up with drift-sand; the inscriptions on the tombs, often a mere charcoal scrawl of some unlettered friend or parent, is soon effaced by winds and rain.

One is wholly unprepared for the appearance of Metlaoui proper. In ten years' time a village has sprung up here, partly of factories and smoky chimneys, but chiefly of trim bungalows, with white walls and red roofs, that are dotted over the uneven surface of the ground. The whole site is owned by the company, and inhabited by its officials and overseers. It has its own church, shops, schools, hospital, workmen's clubs, bakeries, and its air of neatness and well-being contrasts pleasingly with the forsaken landscape all around.

The higher posts are reserved for Frenchmen, but among the lower grades you may find a number of other nationalities; Spaniards and Sardinians—hardiest of white Mediterranean races—as well as some Italians, and not a few Greeks. The manual labour in the mines is performed by Africans.

Not along ago nearly every drop of water for this settlement had to be conveyed from Gafsa on the backs of camels. But the company has now captured a spring at the head of the Seldja gorge, about eight miles distant, which brings a copious flow of water into the place. Thus they have been enabled to plant a great number of trees, but I wish they could be persuaded to adopt a little more variety in their choice of them. One grows tired of the eucalyptus, that doleful and dismal growth, and even of the eternal pepper trees, green as they are; and the results, in a few years' time, would be far more charming if they would take the trouble to copy some of the Algerian municipalities in this respect, or—better still—obtain professional advice from the Agricultural Institute at Tunis, which could furnish them with a large list of ornamental timber and shrubs that would thrive equally well, and convert Metlaoui into a veritable garden city. The plants suffer at first from the strong winds, but they acclimatize themselves by degrees.

Remembering what had been told me of the unsuccessful attempt of the French to appropriate the water springs of Sidi Mansur, near Gafsa, I asked Dufresnoy whether the Arabs had not contested the action of his company at Seldja.

"I should think so!" he said. "They raised the devil. But we are not civil servants here, who must humour the caprices of half a dozen savages: the health of the settlement was dependent on our getting this water, and we took it, *voila!* The great ambition of the company is to fix its people on the spot; to make life here so pleasant for them that they don't want to leave."

"You must find it difficult. The Arabs, I suspect, run back to the desert as soon as they have earned a few francs; and as for the European tradesmen, no doubt they get rich quickly, and then return to their homes again as soon as possible."

"That is exactly what the company manages to avoid. Let them prosper, we say; but slowly. And we succeed."

"How so?"

"By manipulating the rates of merchandise transport. The railway to Sfax belongs to us, and we can regulate prices as it suits us; if we liked, we could choke off all trade. Ah, the company knows its business! Of course, that makes us many enemies; they call it high-handedness and brutality—a concern like ours is bound to expose itself to such remarks— *we* call it common sense. If the railway were not ours, if we were not practically dictators of the country, those Americans, with their immense phosphate importation into Europe, would eat us up; and then these local merchants would lose everything. That is the justification of our so-called tyranny. Are we to have nothing for our risks? Look at this installation of machinery—all built, too, with a view to future aggrandizement: does it strike you as a half-hearted speculation?"

Daring, on the contrary. Here are gargantuan sheds, capable of holding thirty thousand tons of mineral apiece; furnaces, miniature volcanoes, for drying them artificially in winter-time, when the sun's heat is insufficient; all around you a gehenna of mad industrial life, smoke and steam, a throbbing agglomeration of wheels and belts and pistons; there are chains of buckets, filled with phosphates, wandering overhead in endless progression or disappearing sullenly into the bowels of the earth; passionate electric motors; mountains of coal and iron contrivances; railway engines snorting and whistling, or bearing a load of minerals down from the hills to where an army of Arabs will tear them out of the cars to dry, amid clouds of tawny dust. One might well grow crazy at the idea of the primary difficulties involved in grafting upon the desert soil this ordered mechanical efflorescence, this frenzied blossoming of human activity.

What is happening?

They are separating the crude phosphate from its natural impurities; drying, pounding, and loading it upon trains for removal to the sea-board. That is all.

Chapter XIV
PHOSPHATES

A light railway leads up to the hills where the phosphates lie. Here you may see the fiends at work. A legion of wild-eyed, swart and nearly nude creatures are disembowelling the hoary mountain: visions such as this must have floated before Milton's eye when he drew his picture of Mammon, who, with his horde of demons, opened in the hill a spacious wound—

Ransacked the centre, and with impious hands   Rifled the bowels of our mother Earth   For treasure better hid....

The workers are chiefly of three races: Tripolitan, Khabyle (Algerian), and Moroccan; they live in separate clusters among the rocks, each with their peculiar national traits and mode of building; there is hardly a woman among them all.

Besides these tribes a certain proportion of Tunisian Arabs are employed, but they are too weak or timorous to relish underground work; a sprinkling of negroes, as well as some of the hillfolk from the district surrounding Metlaoui, who go by the quaint name of Boujaja.

"Good fellows," said Dufresnoy. "They will slit your throat for a you."

The surface phosphates having already become exhausted, the mineral is now pursued into the dim recesses of the earth. Tunnels are excavated, whence smaller ones radiate in definite directions—all of them sustained by wooden beams; the amount of material to be extracted from a given spot is scientifically fixed; it is shattered by minute blasts of dynamite and, once the trolley cars have carried it away, the wooden supports are removed and these cavities filled up by the collapse of the roof. By this means accidents are forestalled such as that which took place some years ago when, owing to an oversight of some subordinate left in charge, an immense mass of mountain fell in, entombing about three hundred miners, whose bodies are not yet recovered. The ill-fated engineer who was legally responsible for the mishap was in Paris at the time; he returned in all haste. After seeing the mischief, he tried to throw himself into an Arab well, and, baulked of this, lay down at night under a passing train and was decapitated.

They showed me a map of this subterranean world, variously tinted according to the regions already exploited and those yet virgin. It reminded me, with its regular streets and blocks, of some model city in the Far West.

The underground workings here are about thirty kilometres in length. Beside these Metlaoui deposits, the company has begun to attack those of Redeyeff, and will shortly open an assault upon the others at Ain Moulares, which lie near Henchir Souatir, the present terminus of the Feriana line. It employs six thousand men; some of the mineral goes as far as Japan; the output of last year amounted to over a million tons.

One may well be interested in the discoverer of these phosphates, in the man who has revolutionized the trade of Tunisia. He is a veterinary surgeon in the French Army—Monsieur Philippe Thomas.

His record is of the best.

Born in 1843, he has taken part in twelve military campaigns, distinguishing himself particularly in the Franco-Prussian war.

But, above all, he is a savant.

He has written valuable treatises on the diseases of domestic beasts, describing, among other things, a hitherto unobserved infectious malady of goats. He is the author of a number of memoirs on the geology of Northern Africa, and has discovered no less than two hundred new species of fossil animals of that country; he has made numerous contributions to our knowledge of its ethnology, prehistoric tombs, and flint implements. Many of these writings date from the seventies and earlier; they have procured for him the membership of learned societies, as well as medals and decorations of all kinds.

A man of such distinction, one would think, coming to Tunisia in 1885 at the head of a scientific expedition sent by the Ministry of Public Instruction, would be received according to his merits. It was far otherwise. Whether from distrust of his capacities or some other cause, Monsieur Cambon, the Resident, assumed towards him a most chilling official manner, and the commanding military officer, General Boulanger, all but refused to grant the escort necessary for his expedition. In one of his papers he speaks of this reception as "several degrees below zero."

Then, in the same year, appeared his sensational report of the discovery of phosphate deposits which he had traced over a long line of country; realizing their commercial value, he insisted that they should be exploited "***pour le plus grand bien de l'agriculture francaise et algerienne.***" Nevertheless, ten years passed ere a company could be formed, as financiers were diffident about the American competition and the risks of installation in a desert country.

A tardy recognition of his services to the company took the form of a pecuniary grant, in 1904, of fifteen thousand francs—little enough, in all conscience, considering the millions he has gained for them. They further honoured him by changing the name of the station-settlement of Metlaoui into "Philippe-Thomas."

"It's very economical," Dufresnoy observed.

I am glad to think that another place of that name, the mining village, will continue to exist; it would seem a pity to erase from the map the tuneful word Metlaoui, which contains the five vowels in a remarkably small compass....

Dufresnoy tells me that those barren slopes where the mines lie, and where the different races now work together in apparent amity, were once the scene of a sanguinary primitive battle. There is a steep gully at one point, a dry torrent; the Khabyles lived on one side of it, the Tripolitans on the other, and between these two races there occurred, on a starlit night in May, 1905, an affray of unearthly ferocity.

The Khabyles, prudent folk, many of whom had served in the French Army, had long been laying in a store of warlike provisions; their secret was well kept, although it was observed that piles of stones were being collected round their huts, and that a goodly quantity of dynamite and petroleum was missing from the stores; some of them possessed guns and revolvers, the rest were armed with knives, daggers and savage mining gear. They chose a Sunday for the attack, well knowing that the Tripolitans, who are good-natured simpletons, would be least prepared to resist them on that day, and half of them in a state of jollification; and they were so sagacious, that they actually induced a few drunken Tripolitans to insult them, before beginning the conflict. This, they knew, would be counted in their favour afterwards.

Hardly was the night come when they advanced in battle array—the fighting contingent in front; behind them the boys and older men, who kept them supplied with stones and weapons. A well-nourished volley of missiles greeted the Tripolitans, some of whom rushed to the fray, while others took refuge in their huts or with the Moroccans who lived in their own village near at hand. It was now quite dark, but at close quarters the stones began to take effect, and hardly was a man down, than five or six Khabyles ran out of the ranks to finish him off with their knives; others, meanwhile, went to the locked huts and fired them, or burst them open with dynamite.

The explosions and lights began to attract attention in Metlaoui; the whole sky was aflame; there were mysterious bursts of sound, too, and a chorus of wild howls. Something was evidently wrong, up there.

A party of Europeans, accompanied by a small force of local police, went up to the mines to investigate. They found themselves powerless; "keep yourselves out of danger," they were told, "and let us settle our own affairs." The carnage was in full swing; it was hell let loose. Not content with killing, they mutilated each other's corpses, bit off noses, gouged out eyes, and thrust stones in the mouths of the dead; burnt and hacked and slashed each other till sunrise; no element of bestiality was lacking. The wounded crawled away to die in caves, or were carried to nomad camps. The number of the dead was never ascertained; Dufresnoy says "about a hundred," which is probably below the mark, as an eye-witness saw three railway trucks loaded with the slain. To this day they find mouldering human remains, relics of that battle, hidden away in crevices of the rocks.

Although, once roused, the Tripolitans fought like demons, they were worsted—the others were too numerous. They had a brief moment of revenge, however; for during their retreat, on Monday morning, they encountered two young Khabyle boys who had been on absence and were now returning to work at the mines, blissfully ignorant of what was going on. These unfortunate lads were literally torn to shreds.

I confess that, as a spectacle, I should have preferred that night's engagement to anything in modern warfare. It must have been a stupendous exhibition of the ***bete humaine***.

The Khabyles meditated nothing short of a total extirpation of the Tripolitan stock; they sent to the mines of Redeyeff for auxiliaries of their nation, some of whom actually arrived in time for the slaughter; the rest were intercepted on the hill-paths by the police of Gafsa, who had been telegraphically summoned and despatched by special train. And soon afterwards, elated by success, the Khabyles fell foul of the Moroccans and sent word that they meant to fight them too for sheltering Tripolitan fugitives in their huts. The Moroccans were delighted at the prospect; but the management got wind of the project in good time, which was just as well, for the Moroccans are not only the most orderly of the native settlers at the mines, but also by far the strongest and fiercest, and it might have fared ill with the Khabyles. The Tripolitan village has now been moved to another site—a certain number of troops, too, are definitely stationed at Metlaoui.

"As usual," said Dufresnoy, "we came in for the blame. They say that we did not allow the real authors, the Khabyles, to be punished, because they are French citizens, and all the rest of it. Don't believe a word of that. If it had been the Tripolitans, we would have acted just the same; we cannot be bothered with decisions of civil courts, which would have satisfied nobody, besides depriving us, probably, of a number of good workmen. There was a little outcry about this, too: that none of the wounded were treated in our hospital, but carried down to the native *funduk* near the station. 'The hospital,' said our director, 'is for those who are injured in the performance of their duty, and not for bloodthirsty savages.' That's sound—that's military. One cannot afford to be sentimental in this country."

I asked what could possibly be the reason for such a ferocious outbreak of hostility.

"Long-standing animosities of race," he said, "and, as determining cause, *cherchez la femme*"

"But you said that there were no women on the place."

"*Eh bien, cherchez toujours....*"

And then it also occurred to me that among the mass of local literature and newspaper files I had perused in his house there was not a single criticism of this affair. I thought it strange, I said.

He smiled.

"Local politics, my friend! We are obliged to keep the Press well under control, you know. Don't compare Tunisian life with life in England; there is no public opinion here, no idea of fair play. These papers, if they were not subventioned, would print abominations such as no English journalist could conceive; they would alienate our best friends in the long run. The company must take account of things as they are, not as they should be—of Arab savagery, Franco-Tunisian malevolence; of journalistic venality and public credulity. Whoever is not for us is against us. That is why the only papers that dare to criticize our management are those which nobody reads; those, to put it bluntly, which are not worth bribing. For the rest, there is not a writer in the whole country capable of grasping either our aims or our methods; the poor fellows have not had the required education. They only want their mouths stopped."

"That must be more convenient than libel suits; and more economical as well."

"Just so. Above all things, we are bound to consider the interests of our shareholders."

Chapter XV
THE SELDJA GORGE

It is good, after such visions of human infirmity and of death, to ride over the plain to the Seldja gorge, an astonishing freak of nature. I was twice within its towering walls of rock; the first time on horseback, accompanied by a young Tripolitan miner, and in the evening; yesterday again, in the torrid noon, afoot, alone.

You will do well, in every case, to ride as far as the ***bordj***, or rest-house, that stands near the entrance of the cleft, since there are about four wearisome miles of level country to be traversed after leaving Metlaoui. On the first occasion the Tripolitan ran for this whole long stretch beside my horse, which trotted briskly; he amused himself, none the less, in belabouring its hind-quarters with a club to make it go still faster, and I confess to being not scandalized, not inordinately scandalized, at this performance. We grow hard among the implacable desert stones. Besides, it was only a hired beast. Any true lover of animals will understand.

Skirting the foot of the hills that trend along, apparently closed, one suddenly encounters a broad stream-bed with a rivulet meandering down its centre; this is the Seldja-water (***arabice***, Thelja). It issues out of a gateway, hitherto unrevealed; and here you may turn aside from the plain and enter into the heart of the mountains, into a world of nightmare effects. This very portal is fantastic, theatrical; it leads into an arena of riven rocks that might serve as council-chamber for a cloud of Ifrits, and is closed at the further end. There is a second gateway to be passed before you can enter the gorge itself.

The track winds upwards—the whole length of the defile is about three miles—sometimes between walls of rock which are chiselled so smoothly by the gentle waters that one can hardly believe them to be of natural workmanship (and at these points, as a rule, your only path is the stream-bed itself); opening out again into wide amphitheatres, rose-tinted cirques of desolation, where masses of debris, slipped down from the heights, lie prone in Dantesque confusion. There are rock-doves and falcons fluttering about the sunny precipices; cliff-swallows build precarious habitations against the roof of yawning caverns; sandpipers and wagtails skim over the streamlet that glides in a smiling flood across reaches of yellow sand. The charm of water in the waste! This Seldja-brook is a true child of the sun; cold in the morning and evening hours, its restless little heart becomes tepid at midday with the glowing beams.

Spiky reeds and tamarisks trip alongside, and the wild fig thrusts demoniac roots into the crevices; here and there you may see a group of oleasters, descendants, maybe, of the now vanished Roman olive plantations in the plain, or a stunted palm that has shot up from the stone cast away by some passing caravan. For these Oueds are all highways dating from immemorial ages; there is a ceaseless passage of man and animals along them.

We passed numbers of camels, groaning and snorting among the slippery rocks, with the water splashing over their feet; higher up, a large descending flock of sheep, over six hundred of them, completely blocked up the valley. They were being led to the plain below, where, thanks to the recent rains, a succulent but ephemeral crop of green had sprung up. Their owner was a fine Boujaja, some six and a half feet in height, accompanied by a sturdy brood of children: milk-drinkers. The upland pastures could wait, he said. Strange to think that two more showers a year might make settlers of these vagrants.

It was among these rocks that Philippe Thomas first detected the traces of those phosphates that have made his name famous. Tissot, in 1878, already anticipated their discovery.

In point of sheer grandeur, of convulsed stratification and cloven ravine, of terrorizing features, I have seen gorges far finer than this of Seldja. Yet it contains one stretch of superlative beauty—a short defile or canon, I mean, formed of two opposing precipices with a chasm of some thirty yards between them; they wind and curve, parallel to one another, with such magisterial accuracy that one would think they had been designed with mighty compasses from on high, and then carved out, sagaciously, by some titanic blade.

Here we halted; it was time to turn back. There was an indentation in the rocks near at hand, fretted away by hungry floods of the past and overhung, now, with creepers and drooping fernery, concerning which my Tripolitan companion told me a long and complicated legend. This shadowy hollow, he explained, was the bridal couch, in olden days, of an earthly maiden and her demon-lover. He was a simple fellow, unfortunately, who knew the story too well to be able to tell it coherently.

On my second visit, however, I pushed vigorously up the stream-bed in the heat of the morning, determined to reach the head of the waters. Gradually the aspect of the valley changes. It opens out; the rocks melt away into bare white dunes, the country assuming the character of a tableland; you begin to feel a sense of aloofness.

There was blazing sunshine in these upper regions, but a fresh breeze; this is the Ras el-Aioun, where the French have bridled some of the wild waters, thrusting them into a tube that carries them in a mad whirl to their settlement at Metlaoui. Here, too, they have planted a promising youthful oasis, a kind of nursery garden of poplars and cypresses and tamarisks and mimosas, in whose shade grow geraniums, mesembryanthemum and other flowers and creepers, as well as a host of vegetables of every kind. I soon discovered a recess in this delectable pleasaunce, and began my solemn preparations for luncheon.

Out of the pool below there resounded a tuneful croaking of frogs: it spoke of many waters....

Presently an Italian workman or gardener with curly grey hair and moustache—the ubiquitous Italian—came up and began to talk,—*per fare un po' di compania*. He conversed delightfully, a smile playing about his kindly old face. He told me about the garden, about the French engineers, about himself, chiefly about himself, in limpid, child-like fashion. He had travelled far in the Old and New Worlds; in him I recognized, once again, that simple mind of the wanderer or sailor who learns, as he goes along, to talk and think decently; who, instead of gathering fresh encumbrances on life's journey, wisely discards even those he set out with.

Seldja, he told me, used to be a dangerous place for Europeans to traverse; many robberies and even murders had taken place there in times past; the new regime, of course, had put an end to all that. But there were still two perils: the frightful flies that bred diseases and made the gorge almost impassable in the hot months (every one suffered from fevers), and the serpents. Ah, those *maladette bestie di serpenti*—they swarmed among the rocks: they were of every kind and size; worst of all, the spleenful naja. He himself had killed one that measured two metres in length and was as thick as a man's arm. They don't wait till you can hit them, he said, but rush straight at you, swift as an arrow, upraised on their massive posterior coils, hissing like a steam-engine, and swelling out their throat with diabolical rage.

This is the beast that figured in the competition between Aaron and Pharaoh's conjurers, and it remains the favourite of modern African snake-charmers, who catch it after first irritating it by means of a woollen cloth wherein the fangs are embedded and broken. It is also, no doubt, the dreaded species which Sallust describes as infesting the region of Gafsa. But Lucan goes a little too far in his account of Cato's expedition into these parts; this veracious historian has inserted a few pages of sublime serpent nonsense, exquisite fooling....

Of all the deadly worms that breed in these wildernesses the most formidable, because the most sluggish, is the two-horned nocturnal cerastes, the "pretty worm of Nilus." No sensible person, nowadays, goes into the bled[1] in summer-time unless armed with a phial of the antidote—Trousse Calmette or Trousse Legros—whose liquid is injected with a hypodermic syringe above and below the wound, and has saved many lives.

"And the scorpions, Signore! We have to tie cotton-wool round the legs of our beds so that these infernal creatures cannot climb up while we are asleep; they get entangled in it, ha, ha! And that is why we all keep cats and hens, who eat them, you know, just like the Arabs do. And sometimes it rains scorpions."

I had heard that story before, from natives; and it may well be founded on fact. The terrific gusts of desert wind overturn the stones under which the scorpions lie; the fragile beasts are exposed to the blast and, being relatively light, swept skyward

---

1 This is one of the many Arabic words which admit of no clear translation. As opposed to a town, it means a village or encampment; as opposed to that, the open land, a plain, or particular district. When colonists talk of "going into the bled," they mean their farms; in newspaper language it signifies the country generally, inhabited or not—what we should call "the provinces "; oftentimes, again, the barren desert or (more technically) the soil.

across leagues of country with the flying sand. A similar explanation has been given for those old accounts of frog and fish rains.

"Yes; they drop from the clouds. During certain storms I have picked them off my clothes, three or four at a time. Rather a ticklish operation, sir."

So we discussed the world in that umbrageous shelter, to the music of the frogs. He condescended to partake of a microscopic share of my meal, and thereafter left me, with some old-world compliment, to irrigate his thirsty lettuces.

Chapter XVI
AT THE HEAD OF THE WATERS

I sat alone, screened from the midday heat, drowsy and content. It was a pleasant resting-place, under that leafy arbour, through which only a few rays of light could filter, weaving arabesque designs that moved and melted on the floor as the wind stirred the foliage overhead. And a pleasant occupation, listening to those amiable amphibians in the mere below—they carried my thought back to other frog-concerts, dimly remembered, in some other lands—and gazing through the green network of branches upon that sun-scorched garden, where now a silvery thread of water began to attract my attention as it stole, coyly, among the flower-beds.

The day is yet young, methought; it is too hot to think of marching home at this hour. Now is the time, rather, for a pipe of *kif*—if only to demonstrate the difference that exists between man and the ape. For your monkey can be taught to eat and drink like a Christian; he can even learn to smoke tobacco. But he cannot smoke *kif*: the stuff would choke him.

Four pipes, reverentially inhaled ... it was almost too much, for a mere dilettante.

But the mystery of the frogs, the when and where of it, was solved. Slowly and benignly the memories travelled back, building themselves into a vision so clear-cut and elaborate withal, that I might have been holding it, as one holds some engraving or miniature, in my hand. It was in the Rhine-woods, of course; long years ago, in summertime. But the frog-music here was not amiable at all; never have I heard such angry batrachian vociferations. They came in a discontented and menacing chorus from ten thousand leathery throats, and almost drowned our converse as we crept along through the twilight of trees that shot up from the swampy earth.

These Rhine-woods are like pathless tropical jungles: everything is so green and luxuriant; and morning grew to midday while we threaded our way through the tangle of interlacing boughs and undergrowth. Yet we knew, all the time, that something else was in store for us, some joy, some surprise. And lo! there was an opening in the forest, and we suddenly found ourselves standing upon the summit of a high bank at whose foot there rolled a sunlit and impetuous torrent. Too staid for the formation of ripples, too swift for calm content, the river seemed to boil up from below in a kind of frolicsome rage. A blissful sight.

"*Er spinnt*" my companion was saying.

In what obscure chamber of the brain had those words slumbered, closely folded, for thirty years? It was indeed an authentic weaving of arabesque designs upon the even texture of the living liquid mass; multitudinous rings and ovals and lozenges were cast up from the green depths as from a mighty over-bubbling cauldron; some fiercely engulfed again, others torn hither and thither into new and pleasing shapes, fresh ones for ever emerging; only a few contrived to linger unchanged, floating in sunny splendour down the face of the waters. A blissful sight! The dark and mazy woodlands, now, were left far behind—the croaking of the frogs sounded strangely distant. We gazed in ecstasy upon that shining flood....

On my return journey down the Seldja gorge, that afternoon, I had a narrow escape. It struck me that it would be more agreeable, instead of once more following the windings of the brook, to proceed along the railway—a single line—that climbs down from Ras-el-Aioun to within a few hundred yards of the **bordj**, where my horse was waiting. It was easier walking; it would also be shadier (in the tunnels) and, last and chiefest, I would enjoy a change of scene by looking down into the valley instead of up at the cliffs.

Plausible reasoning.

This line is a pretty little piece of engineering; there are bridges and steep embankments that afford fine views into the tortuous depths of the gorge; there are tunnels, blasted into the rock without lining of masonry, deliciously cool and all too short—all too short save one, that seemed never-ending. It writhed about, too, in that dark mountain; I saw no speck of light, either before or behind me; the iron roadway was raised about a foot, on rough stones, above the narrow path that followed the jagged, irregular wall of rock along which I was groping and stumbling. Rather an awkward place, I thought, to meet a train——

And as if in that reflection had lain the potency of a spell, there came upon me, at that moment, from behind, a distinct blast of wind and a low rumbling sound. I pricked up my ears. There was no doubt about it: a train, still invisible, was gliding in good-natured fashion, with steam shut off, down the gradient. A considerable number of ideas, incongruous and quite beside the mark, passed through my mind; but also this one—if I ran, I should inevitably stumble against a sleeper or some projecting stone; if I stumbled, I should lose my presence of mind, and then, perhaps—! Meanwhile, the noise grew louder, deafening; already, in imagination, I felt the monster's hot breath upon me.

Walking steadily, therefore, for a few more yards, I felt a little cavity in the rough-hewn wall of rock that appeared deeper than the others; there I compressed myself, feeling flatter than a turbot, and absurdly resigned. It was the nick of time. The earth was trembling under the mechanical horror; it passed me, with a roar and rush of wind, by I know not how many inches; there were flashes of light, a screeching of machinery, an acrid smell of mineral oils and heated metal. Then all was over again, save for a choking-fit produced by a deluge of bituminous coal.

Just a little flutter.

But outside that tunnel, in the sunshine, I sat down and indulged in certain musings. **Suicide of an Englishman in Tunisia**: that was it; inasmuch as even they who know me well could hardly be brought to believe that such an act of abysmal foolishness, as this of not investigating on which side the safety-niches were, could be the result of accident. An ignoble, ridiculous death.

It must have been a fit of temporary obliviousness, brought about by the unaccustomed heat of the sun.

Or possibly the *kif*....

It affects people differently.

I must limit myself to three pipes, in future.

Chapter XVII
ROMAN OLIVE-CULTURE

Now, on the former occasion, instead of descending into the *bordj* from the railway line, I rode with the Tripolitan once more out of the rock-portal into the plain, that glowed with the fugitive fires of sunset. It is a treeless waste, bereft of every sign of cultivation.

And yet, if you look on your left hand as you issue from the gorge, you will perceive, at the very narrowest point, some fragments of ancient masonry adhering to the cliff; they are all that remains of a Roman dam which blocked up the valley, regulated the supply of water flowing from above, and purified it from stones and sand. The inference is clear: the plain must have been cultivated in those days. Likely enough, it was covered, like many other parts of "Africa," with olives, that drew their life from this judiciously managed water-supply.

The Oued Seldja to-day fulfils no such useful function. Once the rock-portal is passed, it unlearns all its sprightly grace and trickles disconsolately through the sands, expiring, at last, in the dreary Chott el Rharsa.

Monsieur Bordereau thinks that the ancient "forest of Africa" was composed chiefly of olive plantations, and proofs of the former abundance of these trees can be found in certain local names, such as Jebel Zitouna—the Mount of Olives—clinging to localities where not a tree is now visible; there are also sporadic oleasters growing near many Roman ruins. Strong evidence; and still stronger is this: that Roman oil-presses have actually been found, buried in the desert sand. Up to a short time ago the Arabs deliberately destroyed the olives, to avoid paying the tax on them; the French have changed all this, and though I am not aware that they go so far as did the Romans, who encouraged tree-planting by exemption from imposts, yet they have inaugurated a severe regime; one reads with satisfaction of exemplary penalties inflicted for illicit timber-cutting.

It is good to remember, also, that whereas the Romans had five centuries of peace to bring Tunisia to its high pitch of prosperity, the French only began yesterday. And they have a harder task before them, for in the interval the Arabs have arrived in the country. It is they, with their roving and pastoral habits, who have done the mischief, changing arable land into pasture, which grows ever poorer, and finally desert. The fertility of these regions may be said to have been annihilated by the goats of a nomad race, whose faith has made it improvident and mentally sterile.[2]

Yet it may be disputed whether the land was as thickly wooded under the Romans as some would have us believe. If so, how was it that after three centuries of their rule there should come a drought lasting for five years? Wood brings water, and if things were so satisfactory, why did they penuriously hive and distribute the element? They described Africa as a "waterless land"; Marius, when he made his forced march across country to surprise Gafsa, took in at one place a sufficient provision of water to last for three days. This, however, may be due to the fact that he purposely kept to the desert lest, by following the main route, his designs should be made public.

One thing strikes me as conclusive evidence that the "Africa" of olden days was a different country: they had no camels. These beasts were unknown there at the time of Julius Caesar, and only came into common usage towards the end of the fourth century. The Africa of to-day, without camels, would be almost uninhabitable.

Some years ago, whilst staying among the magnificent forests of Khroumiria,

---

2   I have just re-perused Lapie's ***Civilizations Tunisiennes***. He says that "la chevre est le genie malfaisant de la Regence.... Plus que le despotisme, plus que le fatalisme, elle a ruine le pays: c'est la chevre, en effet, qui deboise et surtout qui s'oppose au reboisement, et l'on sait quelle influence a eue sur le regime des eaux et sur la fertilite du sol le deboisement de la province d'Afrique." Apropos of this pasturing by nomad cattle, it is a singular fact that whereas a large proportion of desert plants of northern Tunisia are poisonous to camels and goats, here, in the south, nearly all of them are edible.

forests such as certainly never clothed these southern hills, I grew interested in this question of the old African water-supply. Comparing the accounts of classic authors with what has been written by modern students like Bourde, Carton and others, whose very names have faded from my memory, I remember coming to the conclusion—a very obvious one, no doubt—that supposing all the ruined Roman hydraulic contrivances were now in working order, supposing them even to be furnished with such improvements as modern science could suggest, still the French would be unable to obtain, at the present moment, the agricultural results of the Romans. The positive diminution in the supply of liquid has been too great. Archaeologists, for instance, have discovered in the district of Gafsa alone over a hundred Roman wells and reservoirs, of every shape and size; but it would be sheer waste of money to re-activate many of these ancient works—there are wells which would remain dry from one year's end to another; the watercourses, too, have shrunk or altogether expired.

Quite apart from what the French have taken from it, this Seldja brook must have carried down a larger volume of water in those days, helped, as is very probable, by small tributary streamlets which have now ceased to flow.

Old Arab authors say that one used to be able to walk from one end of North Africa to the other in the shade. Allowing for some exaggeration, this means that either the legendary African forest of the Romans continued to subsist, or that certain bare tracts covered themselves with timber in post-Roman periods of abandonment, before the Arabs and their goats had time—for it must have required time—to change the climate and aspect of the province.

These woodlands, at all events, cannot have been all of olives. There is Sbeitla, for instance, the Roman city whose remains I was unable to visit owing to the Arctic blasts of wind; viewed from the railway, its surroundings look so bleak and bare that nobody would believe they could ever have been timbered. Yet, concerning Sbeitla, we happen to possess the testimony of three independent older eye-witnesses, who visited the spot at different periods: first Shaw (about 1725), then Bruce, then the botanist Desfontaines. All three of them describe the region as wooded. And, as if to clinch the matter, Leo Africanus, writing in 1550, says that the inhabitants of Gafsa and its district made their boots out of the skins of stags. (These are no doubt the fortassa deer, a few of which still linger in the country north of Feriana.) Stags can only live in timbered regions. If these forests were still in existence there would be a greater abundance of water; the cold in winter would be less intense, and so would the summer heat, since forests are harmonizers of all climatic discords.

Now these woodlands were not composed of olives, but for the most part of junipers and of Aleppo pines, a precious growth to which the French began to pay attention some five years ago. These bright and graceful trees flourish on the poorest soil and multiply rapidly; they are valuable not only for their timber, but for their turpentine. You can buy, in the Gafsa market, a crude black tar made from this tree; the Arabs use it for impregnating the linings of their water-skins, like the Greeks for their receptacles of rezzinato wine.

The only drawback to these pines is that their inflammable branches are always suggesting a display of extempore fireworks to the Arabs, who are the veriest pyromaniacs.

Chapter XVIII
THE WORK OF PHILIPPE THOMAS

The old olive plantations are creeping back again into regions that have been deserted for centuries. They follow the railway lines; and nothing is a fitter commentary on the medievalism which deplores ***the building of railways into the desert*** than facts like that of the plain of Maknassy—a sterile tract up to a few years ago—which is now covered, for a distance of sixty kilometres, by olive groves. Why? Because the line from Sfax to Gafsa happens to pass through it.

The same will take place in due course along the Feriana and other southern lines, and thus one of the gravest problems that confront the Tunisian administration will be solved: the unstable nomads will fix themselves—they are already fixing themselves—round these new agricultural centres. In 1890 there were still eight tents to every five houses in Tunisia, but this proportion is rapidly changing. And besides this, the railway, with its facility for the rapid conveyance of troops, has given security to regions formerly so dangerous that no settler, however favourable the soil, would have dared to establish his home there; it has awakened the date industry and created halfa deposits all along the line.

There is one of them at Gafsa station, for instance—relatively small; and yet, in the season, two hundred camel-loads of this costly hay arrive there every day, to be dried, pressed and stored ready for transportation to the coast, whence it is shipped to Europe. In 1905 sixteen thousand six hundred tons of halfa were forwarded from the interior by the Sfax-Gafsa line alone!

And were it not for this railway the branch line to Tozeur would never have been contemplated; the oases of Souf and Djerid and Nefzaoua, with their teeming populations, would have slumbered the sleep of ages in their burning desert sands. And to realize what a change it has wrought in the appearance of the ports of Sfax, Sousse and even Tunis, one must have known these places in the olden days. The company pays yearly half a million francs to the Government; it contributes another yearly sum of 600,000 francs towards the harbour enlargement scheme of Sfax; indeed, it may be said to have created the modern town of Sfax, its hotels, banks, restaurants, theatres.

And what brought the railway?

The phosphates. But for their discovery no Utopian would have thought of constructing these lines just yet. An unlovely deposit of brown dust has worked a revolution upon the minds of men, upon the face of the country. It has even enriched the French vocabulary.

"Your friend, is he an *alfatier*?"

"No, sir; he is a *phosphatier*."

As I issued out of the rock-portal of the Seldja gorge and beheld that strip of masonry which told so plain a story, with the now barren plain at its foot, it struck me that this spot was pregnant with a romance beyond that of mere scenery. It was well, here, to pause awhile and contrast old and new notions of African prosperity. The Romans had the same difficulties to contend with as have the French: a harsh climate, and fickle and faithless natives who "cannot be bridled by threats or kindness." They had the same ambitions; so Strabo tells us that they used every endeavour to make settlers of them and fix them to the soil, and "paid particular attention to Masanasses, King of Numidia, because it was he who formed the nomads of civil life and directed their attention to husbandry."

Both administrations are necessarily based on military rule. And if the now uncultivated plain affronts our eye, there is already a set-off to this apparent superiority of the ancient regime in the new line of railway which, at great expense, has been made to climb up the sinuosities of the Seldja gorge itself.

Whither wending?

To fetch more phosphates!

Here they lie, the quintessential relics of those little Eocene fishes and other sea beasts, if such they were, that swam and crawled about the waters many years ago—piled up on terraces so high that the mind grows dizzy at contemplating their multitudes, or the ages required to squeeze them into this priceless powder; piled up for 500 miles along their old sea-beach—an arid inland chain of hills, nowadays, where hardly a blade of grass will grow; sterile themselves, the cause of surpassing fertility elsewhere. These phosphates are something of a symbol: there are men and women fashioned after this model.

I question whether the men of the **Pax Romana** could ever have reached the phosphate-extracting stage. They were not trending in that direction. Eyes were turning inwards, and the age of sober thinking was past and over for the time being, since the Orient began to infect the world with the mephitic vapours of self-consciousness. Truth was a drug in the market; for twenty long centuries the Banu-Israel, with their ferocious contempt of craftsmanship and honest intellectual labour, were enabled to foul the stream of human endeavour. It is gratifying to think how thoroughly the modern Jews have shaken off their ancient bigotry—a good refutation, by the way, of those scholars who still argue about the "immutability of race-characters."

But those earlier and artless Galileans, methinks, must have been on the mental level of the Tripolitan savage running beside my horse: it needs no very cunning marabout to convince him that his little troubles will be set aright in a world hereafter, where he shall sit comfortably enthroned and listen to his enemies gnashing their teeth. For the poor in mind are like children in this, that they create realities to coincide with emotional states; and for such as these, they say, is the kingdom of Heaven reserved.

Nevertheless, though men sought the "inner light" and not phosphate deposits in those days, yet certain men of God, roaming about these same stony wildernesses, made discoveries in natural history no less surprising than that of Monsieur Philippe Thomas. Saint Anthony encountered a faun—half-man, half-goat; he spoke to the creature and was charmed by its edifying discourse. You will object that Saint Anthony is known to have been a hallucinated neyropathe; that the story, therefore, may not be true. So be it.

But such a description can hardly be applied with decency to certain holier and wiser men, who saw with their own eyes things yet stranger. The great Augustin tells his congregation—it is in one of his sermons, I believe—that in these deserts there are men without heads, men who have one single eye placed in the centre of their breasts. You may suggest that the saint was quoting from the heathen pages of Herodotus, the **_Father of Lies_**. Nothing of the kind. He is too conscientious to speak from hearsay of such marvellous matters; he says that he personally went among these headless monocular folk; he says that he spoke to them and lived with them; that he made a study of their morals and social institutions, which, in this particular sermon, he holds up as an example to his two-eyed Christian hearers.

And Saint Augustin has the reputation of being a fairly truth-loving saint and **_doctor ecclesiae_**.

No; phosphate-hunting was assuredly out of the question under such conditions; scientific curiosity and commercialism, parents of fair talk and fair dealing among men, retire discomfited when there are immortal souls to be saved. And soon enough they came, those Ages of Faith, of moral dyspepsia and perverse aspirations, when truth-seeking, useless under the **_Pax Romana_**, became much worse than useless—perilous, that is, to life and limb. So quickly do we forget past torments, that some of us continue to yearn for those picturesque days of burnings and thumb-screwings.

Meanwhile, if truth is found useful for the moment, it is due to the humanizing work of those quiet investigators like Philippe Thomas—to the men who have armed their country for the heroic task of cleansing the Augean stables.

Monsieur Dufresnoy had never met the phosphate discoverer, but another gentleman described him as follows:—

"He is a simple fellow, and the devil for work. Married, and a good husband; clear eyes; spectacles, a short beard, rather stout, and not dark; never so happy as when he is examining old bones and trash of that kind. A **_bon garcon_**, mind you. And yet—Lord! what a simpleton. He could have become a millionaire if he had managed the thing properly. Too modest, perhaps—too unworldly; too foolish, or too proud: who can tell?

"You never know what is going on in the minds of these **_savants_**. He told them he was a veterinary surgeon, and not a man of business. Can you understand such an attitude?"

"I must think about it, Monsieur."

And so I did, riding home that evening from the Seldja gorge—and next day too; but, somehow or other, have not yet attained a mature opinion on the subject.

It may be, however, that there is nothing to prevent a man from being simultaneously modest and proud—nothing, save the fact that we have not yet coined a word for an alloy of these particular ingredients. We have words, always either too few or too many; words which are for ever emancipating themselves from our control and becoming masters instead of slaves, so that our ideas, which ought to be formed by independent cerebration, are half derived from mere verbal symbols, which become a kind of intellectual pepsine that weakens the strongest systems. So when we speak of a man being "proud," that miserable expression is apt to engross and dominate us, conjuring up an image which excludes certain others: that of modesty, for instance.

It comes to this, that if we wish to describe a man who does not seem to fit into any of the categories permitted by ordinary words, we are driven to refer him to some exemplar recognized in legend or history—we talk of his being Epicurean, Voltairean, and so forth.

Let us say, therefore, that Monsieur Thomas, like Pasteur, is of the Promethean type—a seeker after verity, a light-bringer.

POSTSCRIPT.—This is surely a land of coincidences. In a Tunisian paper of this very morning I read of the death, on the 13th of February, of Monsieur Thomas. It describes him as "one of the most perfect citizens of our poor humanity." He only lived a year to enjoy the annuity of six thousand francs which the Government of the Regency, with belated thoughtfulness, had granted him.

Chapter XIX
OVER GUIFLA TO TOZEUR

A mule, a sturdy beast, was waiting to convey me from Metlaoui to Tozeur. Leaving my heavier baggage to follow with some camels, I rode into the dawn.

Considerably less than half-way stands the rest-house of Guifla, kept by an Algerian with a pretty wife. Here I saw a few carved Roman stones which had been found, the man told me, in the neighbouring Oued Baghara. At Guifla, according to Valery Mayet, they killed an ostrich twenty years ago—a *rara avis* in these parts.

There were numbers of engineers and workmen at this place, engaged in laying down the line of railway which will unite Tozeur to Metlaoui. It cannot help being a paying concern, I should think, to judge by the traffic that passed me in the course of this day, for I was hardly ever out of sight of a caravan.

It was an ideal day for desert travelling—a grey, sunless sky, a gentle breeze. Another weary stretch brings one to El-Hamma, a small oasis fed by hot springs which the Romans long ago utilized, and where I had hoped to refresh myself with a Turkish bath. Alas! the hammam is only a shallow tank covered with palm-thatching; there were some twenty Arabs splashing about this establishment and soaping themselves and their boy-children—bathing was out of the question. Near at hand lies the women's bath, which is built on the same primitive lines. A pious legend runs to the effect that this water of El-Hamma used to be cold, but an Arab marabout was persuaded to spit into it and, lo! it suddenly became hot and mineral....

As you approach Tozeur the landscape becomes more desert-like; mountains are left behind; stones are rarer; you wade in sand. One realizes how useless it would be to construct a good road in these parts, since every storm would drown it. And such storms are sometimes of great force; there was a celebrated one in 1857 which lasted for seventy-two hours. It threw some of the riders of a French detachment off their horses, and finally obliged the whole company to stamp up and down for twenty-four hours in the twilight of raging sand for fear of being buried alive. It submerged several hundred palm trees of the Tozeur oasis **_up to their crowns_** (they are 60 to 100 feet high).

Notwithstanding these difficulties, an enterprising Maltese runs a motor-car from Metlaoui to Tozeur and Nefta for all such persons as are prepared to pay his price, and I hear that the speculation has paid well. There were moments during my ride when I regretted not having come to some understanding with him; when I grew tired of the jolting mule, the rough track and an Arab saddle which keeps one's legs at an angle of 179 degrees. True, my conveyance had only cost four francs....

Straining my eyes at the water-shed beyond El-Hamma, whence one has the first view of Tozeur and its palm forest, I thought to detect, at an immeasurable distance, two minute dusky streaks, swimming in air—other oases, no doubt. They seemed to dangle, by some gossamer thread, from the grey vault of Heaven.

This first view of the oasis of Tozeur, and the Chott Djerid beyond it, has often been praised. To me, arriving at the water-shed on a cloudy afternoon, that line of inky-black palm trees with its background of blanched sterility melting into a lowering, leaden-hued sky, conveyed a most uncanny impression: the prospect was absolutely familiar! Yes, there was no doubt about it: I had seen the place before; not in Africa, of course, but—somewhere else. Where—where? Suddenly I remembered: it was a northern landscape, a well-known forest of sombre firs, rising out of the wintry plain. The white, salty expanse, filling up the interstices between the palms, helped to complete the illusion; it was powdered snow among the tree-tops. For a brief moment I was **_transported_**....

It was not long before I found a companion at Tozeur. He was an Arab from the Souf, region of sand; dark-skinned, oval-faced, with straight eyelashes, straight nose, and an infectious, lingering smile; quite a worthless fellow; he had picked up a few words of French slang, and never tired of exhibiting them. We rode out to the Chott to see the extraction of the salt, which is a Government monopoly; the track leads past a famous lotus, a Methuselah among trees, whose shadow covers 120 square metres of ground and whose branches are so long, so weary with age, that they bend downward and touch the earth with their elbows—to rest, as it were—and then rise up again, refreshed. These salines are about three miles from Tozeur and an uncommonly simple establishment; they dig a ditch in the morass which promptly fills with water; the liquid evaporates, leaving the salt, which impregnates it, to be piled up in heaps on dry land. Next, they stow the mineral in sacks and transport it to Tozeur on donkeys. It undergoes no preparation whatever, but is sold as it comes out of the Chott, agreeable to the palate though rather yellowish in colour. Needless to say the Government runs no risk of the supply failing; there is salt, a swooning stretch of salt, as far as eye can reach.

Once you have issued from the oasis in this direction it is all a level of dried-up mud, speckled with low shrubs and dangerous watery spots, where a man may slowly sink down and disappear for ever. A strange desert lily, purple and golden, starts leafless, like a tall orchid, out of the bitter waste; camels eat its fat, bulbous, snowy-white root; the Arabs call it **tethuth**.

I saw some darker markings on the surface of the expanse which the workman at the salines declared to be the ruins of old buildings and quite inaccessible nowadays, but they may well have been small ridges of sand, magnified by mirage: those oasis-Arabs have rather indifferent eyesight. Plainly visible, however, was a line of palms about eight miles distant to the east; it was one of a group of oases of Oudiane. I looked at it, wondering whether I should pass that way on my homeward journey.

But my companion, with a languishing gesture, pointed in the other direction, towards his home.

Tozeur, he thought, was all very well, and so were Oudiane and all the rest of them, but Eloued was fairer by far. And only three days' journey! Why not leave this country and go to the Souf, to Eloued, instead? **Sacre nom!** I could return by way of Biskra if I liked. And if I paid him five francs for a camel he would accompany me the whole way, like a brother. The five francs, he explained, were only for camel-hire; he did not want me to pay for his food; he liked me for my company—it seems I reminded him, in a way, of the folks at Eloued. They must be charming people, and I was almost tempted to follow his advice and make their acquaintance.

Later on we went to what they call the Roman *barrage* of the main oasis river; the large blocks of which it is composed are unquestionably antique, but they have been carried to this spot not by the ancients, but by Berber cultivators of long ago. Gazing upon these venerable stones we were led to talk of past times, of buried treasures and their wondrous lore. One of his uncles, he tells me, is versed in the black arts and an adept at raising hoards; he learnt it from a Moroccan. But bad luck had dogged his footsteps lately. He discovered a treasure whose guardian *jin* offered to surrender it if he brought three things: a white goat, certain materials for fumigation, and "the book." It seemed a very simple request, but each time, unfortunately, that he arrived at the enchanted spot, he found that, for some extraordinary reason, he had left at home one or the other of these three articles; and when at last he managed to bring all three of them together, he accidentally—*sale bete!*—said a pious "bismillah" at the critical moment, which of course spoilt everything.

And here a wild craving came upon me: I wished to follow the winding of this brook and trace it to its source, which I judged to be not far distant. The companion, smiled, as usual; he was ready for anything; but the undertaking proved to be rather arduous. We walked and climbed for long among the gardens, crawling under vines and thorny shrubs, wading tributary brooks and clambering up and down their steep earthen banks with a hundred dogs in full pursuit; there was no possibility of orientation; we doubled our tracks over and over again—it was like being imprisoned in the works of a clock.

At last, and doubtless by the merest of accidents, we emerged from the true oasis of orderly fruit trees and vegetables; the soil became sandy and uneven, with palms sprouting up in isolated clusters amid tamarisks and bristly reeds. The stream, meanwhile, continued to divide and subdivide into smaller rivulets. After a good deal of walking on this kind of ground, we finally reached the head of the waters—the eye, as the Arabs poetically call a fountain, alluding to its liquid purity, its genial play of light and movement.

It trickles out under a tall incline of sand, and the crowns of the palms at this spot are not quite on a level with the desert overhead. Looking down from these sandy heights, I found that we had followed a tortuous river of green palms, that flowed through yellow sands into a distant lake of the same green—the oasis.

But the companion had become quite silent. He was bewitched, apparently, by the rural charms of this place. At last he said:

"If only I had brought some *kif* to smoke!"

Your Oriental, as a rule, becomes hungry at the sight of a fair landscape; he manifests a sudden yearning for food. Not so these Souafa; they must have their native *kif* on such occasions. They are all, I am sorry to say, partakers of the pernicious drug.

"You have forgotten your *kif*?" I asked. "Well, that *was* an oversight!"

And, to his astonishment, I fumbled in my pocket, produced the stuff and lit a pipe. I smoked on placidly, looking at him and wondering what his thoughts might be. "An Inglis"—perhaps he was saying to himself—"one of those who joke and talk in such friendly fashion, and then, when it cornes to a you's worth of *kif*—a single puff of his pipe...! **Sacre cochon!** That is how they grow rich."

Possibly he reasoned thus, but I fancy he reasoned not at all. There he sat, and kept his eyes fixed on the ground; a European might have feigned interest in something else, or cheerful indifference, but this desert-child did none of these things. He simply sat and suffered dumbly: it was a blow of fate, to be borne like all the rest of them. A fine exemplar (**edition mignonne**) of the mektoub profession. It gave a dignity to the fellow.

Presently I made him a gift of the whole apparatus. He was quite speechless, at first, with surprise.

The spot was well chosen for indulgence in the divine herb, bland quencher of doubts, begetter of blissful images; impossible to conceive anything but a good genius residing amid these bubbling waters and gently stirring foliage. Everything was kindly and gracious, and yet——

"Yonder," he said, pointing dreamily with his pipe-stem to a place not far distant, "yonder they killed a man and a woman. They hacked them to little pieces."

And he unfolded a tale of love and revenge.

It was the usual intrigue; with this peculiarity, that the woman was quite a poor creature, of blameless past, married and mother of children; the man—though what we should call a "gentleman by birth"—had long ago become a vagabond, a child of iniquity, an outcast from the coast-towns, whom some wave of misfortune had left stranded on this green island in the desert. Listening to the hazy and rather disconnected recital, I tried to piece the story together as it really happened; to discover its logic, its necessity; the arts by which this decayed citizen, proficient only in the lore of vice and scorned by the whole populace, had gained his end; above all, how it came about that these two never wearied of their infatuation. Had he struck some latent and hideously defective chord in her motherly breast, that began to throb in response to his amorous complexities—was ***that*** their common bond?

Likely enough.

But I would prefer to think otherwise. I would prefer to think that this woman's very simplicity, and this green dell, had worked a miracle; purging and simplifying him, carrying him away from depraved memories of middle life towards certain half-forgotten and holier ideals of youth that revived, at last, and took shape in the prime features of this—as he may have called it—pastoral diversion; making him cling to them stubbornly, even as we might promise ourselves to cling to some friend of past days, were he ever to return....

The idyll lasted for long, ere the awful retribution came—the element of insecurity acting, I suppose, as a cement. There is in most of us, Arabs or otherwise, a deep-seated sporting instinct (is that the right word?) which the system of legalized unions was contrived to curb, but cannot; if connubial life were a hazardous liaison there would be fewer divorces.

A perverse and sordid romance, you will say.

And yet it endured, like many of its kind.

Chapter XX
A WATERY LABYRINTH

Tozeur is more than twice as large as Gafsa, and the inhabitants are a healthier race, good-natured and docile, with much of the undiluted Berber blood still in their veins. The houses are also of better construction, and not a few of them can boast of cool, vaulted chambers and an upper story. Unfortunately for the artistic effect, new French buildings are rising up here and there; it is inevitable—the place cannot be expected to stand still; artists and dreamers must now go further afield.

And the oasis is a forest of sumptuous splendour, wherein grow bananas (absent in Gafsa), together with every other kind of fruit and vegetable, but chiefly date-palms, that give the highest and most constant return. They cultivate seventy different varieties. There are half a million trees paying taxes—the common variety sixty centimes, the delicate amber-tinted and translucent ***deglat*** twice as much; some trees produce more than fifty francs a year. But they require incessant care; "palms must eat and drink," say the Arabs; they drink, in the summer months, a hundred cubic metres of water apiece!

The export of these dates has been going on for centuries; in 1068 the geographer Bekri wrote that almost every day a thousand camels, or even more, leave Tozeur loaded with dates, and the trade will become still livelier when they have finished building the railway which is to connect this place with the present terminus Metlaoui. Maybe the Egyptians introduced the tree into these regions: they cultivated dates as early as 3000 B.C. It is perhaps the earliest fruit of which we have clear record, save that old apple of 4004 B.C. which gave some trouble to Adam and Eve.

In olden days they sold negro slaves here for two or three quintals of dates apiece.

The irrigation of these palms is a hair-splitting business. Water-conduits, varying in size from a brook to the merest runlet, cross and recross each other on palm-stem aqueducts at different levels; the properties are served with the precious element according to time. And inasmuch as the labourers have no clocks or watches, they have devised a complicated and apparently frivolous system of marking the hours; the water is cut off from a certain property, for instance, when a certain shadow shall have attained the length of three footsteps of a man, and so forth; the shadow varies according to the seasons, but, in the long run, everybody is satisfied. There is peace now under the palms; the days are over when the lean and hungry desert folk, who cannot climb trees, used to ride hither and, pointing their guns at the terrified cultivators, make them clamber aloft and throw down a month's provision of dates.

Arabs will tell you that there are 194 water springs at Tozeur; they are ready to give you the names of every one of them, and several more; these unite to form what might almost be called a river, which is then artificially divided into three rivulets—divided so neatly, says an old writer, that even some fragment of wood or other object drifting down the current is split up, perforce, into three equal parts, one for each of them; these three, later on, are once more subdivided into seven smaller ones apiece—twenty-one in all; and these, again, into a certain fixed number of almost microscopic brooklets. Allah is all-knowing! To me, wandering for the first time in this region, the irrigation canals seemed to flow from every point of the compass. I teased my spirit with the imaginary task of unperplexing the liquid maze, of drawing a map of this daedal network of intersecting waters.

You can stroll in every direction along shady paths in the oasis and never weary of its beauty. The tiller-folk are a happy people—one can see from their faces that they have few cares; those that are not at work under the trees may be seen splashing about the brooks or wending to market with donkeys that almost disappear under immense loads of green stuff; they will greet you with a smile and a "Bon soir, Moussie!" (It is always bon *soir*.)

Seven little villages nestle under the palms; here and there, too, you enter unexpectedly upon gem-like patches of waterless, shimmering sand—mock-Saharas, golden and topaz-tinted, set in a ring of laughing greenery; there are kingfishers in arrowy flight or poised, like a flame of blue, over the still pools; overhead, among the branches, a ceaseless cooing of turtle-doves. At this season, a Japanese profusion of white blossoms flutters in the breeze and strews the ground; these peaches, apricots, plums and almonds are giants of their kind, and yet insignificant beside the towering trunks of the palms whose leaves shade them from the sunny rays; the fruit trees, in their turn, protect the humble corn and vegetables growing at their feet.

During the Turkish period these oases were in danger of their lives; the sand invaded them, choking up the waters and gradually entombing the plants. The nomads and their flocks and camels, pasturing at liberty round the cultivated tracts, had destroyed the scrub vegetation which hindered the flying desert sands from penetrating into the groves; they had trampled to powder the soil at these spots, so that every breath of wind raised it heavenwards in a cloud. But the peril is averted now by the system of *__tabias__* or sand-dykes introduced some twenty years ago—introduced, I believe, in accordance with the suggestion of Monsieur Baraban, whose book on Tunisia drew attention, among other things, to this deplorable condition of the oases and the threatened loss to the exchequer.

Now, if you look closely at this sand, you will see that it is full of minute crystalline particles, and that, in places where it lies undisturbed, these hard and jagged grains wedge themselves into the softer ones and form a coherent crust. It was observed that the wind cannot raise this crust, and the problem how to manufacture it in the neighbourhood of the oases was solved by enclosing the near-lying tracts of half-desert within low mounds crowned by upright palm branches, and forbidding all access to man and beast. The flying plague heaps itself against the palisade and submerges it; a new set of branches is then inserted, and so the structure grows higher and more efficacious every year. The soil within the enclosures, meanwhile, grows hard; wild shrubs sprout up to help in the work, and though the crust yields, like thin ice, at the slightest pressure of the fingers, the end is accomplished.

The protected districts are already assuming a different aspect from the true desert outside, which shifts with the breeze; apart from their tufts of vegetation, the soil has become quite dark in colour. Only the most reckless of nocturnal nomads will dare to violate these hallowed precincts in search of firewood; the citizens have already learned to regard them with reverential fear. At a long distance from the town I asked a small boy to climb over the palisade.

"Not if you give me a packet of cigarettes!" he said. "The **brigadier**"—in an awed whisper—"he sees everything."

Hearing that protective works of a new kind are being carried on at this moment, I walked yesterday to the bare slopes that lead down to the water-springs. A hundred or more Arabs were engaged, under the supervision of a keen-eyed young Frenchman, in digging a multitude of curved concentric ditches across the hollow of the catchment area, intersected by diagonal ones here and there; the general appearance of the work—the bright yellow of the newly excavated part set against the dark ground of the old—was as if some gigantic fishing-net had been carelessly thrown across the country. These little dykes were about two feet deep, and there must have been already some twenty miles of them. The overseer explained:

"You see what happens. Our putting this tract under the tabia-system had prepared us an unpleasant surprise. The rain formerly used to sink into the soft sand, but since the crust has formed, thanks to our efforts, it no longer sinks, but runs over the hard surface, pours in a flood down that steep incline at whose foot the fountains issue, and threatens to suffocate them with soil torn from its banks. The very life of the oasis was imperilled by our well-meant artifices. But now, with these little ditches, we hope to catch and tame the showers, and force them to wander about in these channels till they either sink into the earth or evaporate. Not a drop of liquid is to leave the catchment basin; it is exactly the reverse of what we desire in Europe."

It struck me as a simple and efficient device.

Midday came and the workers were paid off, each of them receiving a slip of printed paper for the half-day's work; the possession of four of these slips entitles them to exemption from the yearly tax of two francs forty centimes which they would otherwise pay: a good example of the "politique d'association." They trooped away gleefully, and I could not help remarking on their cheerful humour.

"They are gentle as young girls," he said, "and far more tractable; thievish, of course, and untruthful—but so are all children! They attach themselves to me in a pathetic, dog-like fashion, without hope of preferment or any ulterior object.... Yes, they have established themselves in my heart, somehow or other; perhaps because

I am an orphan and rather lonely and susceptible.... I really love these poor Arabs, as a father might love them——"

"That stick of yours: it looks business-like. May I ask whether you ever chastise them?"

"Why not? Would I not thrash my own children if they deserved it? This work in Africa," he went on, "attracts and interests me. At home I lose my personality and become a sheep in a herd, but here, in the desert, I can create and leave a mark, which has always been my ambition. I think I could live in this country for ever. Can you understand such a feeling? None of my colleagues can; their minds are in France, and they complain of a colonial exile, as if Tunisia were the Devil's Island; they call me an enthusiast, because I think well of this warm, palpitating soil in which I seem, I don't know how, to have struck deep roots."

And he gazed lovingly over the sea of glossy palm-tops, down yonder, on our right. This, I thought, was a most unusual type of Frenchman; and yet there was something in his language, or perhaps in his ideas, which was already familiar to me.

"To be Sultan of Tozeur, for example—ha! I would bend them to my will; I would lead them to battle and give them laws; I would have them about me as slaves and companions—they should sing to me and tell me stories while I go to sleep. This fair land seems like the realization of some old, dimly remembered dream of mine. How does it all come about, I wonder?"

Sultan of Tozeur—that gave me the cue, and I hazarded the guess that he had inherited his tastes from certain old rovers and conquerors of the northern seaboard.

"True," he said, "our family comes from Normandy, though we have lived in Paris for two generations. Now how on earth did you find that out?"

These are the men whom the Franco-Tunisian administration will do well to encourage as officials and settlers in the wilder parts.

Chapter XXI
OLD TISOUROS

There is a daily recurring spectacle at Tozeur which enchanted me: the camping ground at dawn. Here the caravans repose after their desert journeys; hence they start, at every hour, in picturesque groups and movement. But whoever wishes for a rare impression of Oriental life must go there before sunrise, and wait for the slow-coming dawn. It is all dark at first, but presently a sunny beam flashes through the distant palms, followed by another, and yet another—long shafts of yellow light travelling through the murk; then you begin to perceive that the air is heavy with the smoke of extinguished camp-fires and suspended particles of dust; the ground, heaving, gives birth to dusky shapes; there are weird groans and gurglings of silhouetted apparitions; and still you cannot clearly distinguish earth from air—it is as if one watched the creation of a new world out of Chaos.

But even before the sun has topped the crowns of the palms, the element of mystery is eliminated; the vision resolves itself into a common plain of sand, authentic camels and everyday Arabs moving about their business—another caravan, in short....

And at midday?

Go, at that hour, to the thickest part of the grove; then is the time; it must be the prick of noon, for the slanting lights of morning and eve are quite another concern; only at noon can one appreciate the incomparable effects of palm-leaf shadows. The whole garden is permeated with light that streams down from some undiscoverable source, and its rigid trunks, painted in a warm, lustreless grey, are splashed with an infinity of keen lines of darker tint, since the sunshine, percolating through myriads of sharp leaves, etches a filigree pattern upon all that lies below. You look into endless depths of forest, but there is no change in decorative design; the identical sword-pattern is for ever repeated on the identical background, fading away, at last, in a silvery haze.

Here are no quaint details to attract the eye; no gorgeous colour-patterns or pleasing irregularities of form; the frosted beauty of the scene appeals rather to the intelligence. Contrasted with the wanton blaze of green, the contorted trunks and labyrinthine shadow-meanderings of our woodlands, these palm groves, despite their frenzied exuberance, figure forth the idea of reserve and chastity; an impression which is heightened by the ethereal striving of those branchless columns, by their joyous and effective rupture of the horizontal, so different from the careworn tread of our oaks and beeches.

Later on, when the intervening vines and fruit trees are decked in leaves, the purity of this geometrical design will be impaired....

The origin of Tozeur is lost in the grey mists of antiquity, since a site like this must have been cultivated from time immemorial; the first classical writer to mention the town is Ptolemy, who calls it Tisouros; on Peutinger's Tables it is marked "Thusuro." The modern settlement has wandered away from this ancient one which now slumbers—together, maybe, with its hoary Egyptian prototype—under high-piled mounds whereon have arisen, since those days, a few mediaeval monuments and crumbling maraboutic shrines and houses of more modern date, patched together with antique building blocks and fragments of marble cornices: an island of sand and oblivion, lapped by soft-surging palms.

They call it Bled-el-Adher nowadays, and this is the place to spend the evening. I was there yesterday, perhaps for the last time.

It exhales a soporific, world-forgotten fragrance. There is no market here, no commercial or social life, save a few greybeards discussing memories on some doorstep; the only mirthful note is a swarm of young boys playing hockey on the sandheaps, amid furious yells and scrimmages.

True hockey being out of the question on account of the deep sand, they have invented a variant, a simple affair: they arrange themselves roughly into two parties, and the ball is struck into the air with a palm branch from the one to the other; there, where it alights, a general rush ensues to get hold of it, clouds of sand arising out of a maze of intertwining arms and legs. The lucky possessor is entitled to have the next stroke, and the precision and force of their hitting is remarkable; they evidently do little else all day long.

I noticed an element of good humour and fair play not prevalent among the Gafsa boys; there was no peevish squabbling, and I only saw one fight which was a perfectly correct transaction—nobody interfering with the two combatants who hammered lustily at each other's faces, and at last separated, satisfied and streaming with blood.

For some days past they had seen my interest in the game, and yesterday I observed that it was suddenly suspended; a consultation was taking place, and presently one of the boys approached me and politely asked whether I would not care to join; if so, I might have his club; and he placed the weapon and ball in my hand. The proposition tempted me; it is not every day that one is invited in such gentlemanly fashion to wallow on all fours with young Arabs. I made one or two strokes, not amiss, that called forth huge applause; and then returned, rather regretfully, to my sand-heap, to meditate on my own misspent youth, a subject that very rarely troubles me.

There is a tall, round building that stands within a hundred yards of where I sat; they call it the "Roman" tower, and the foundation-stones, though not *in situ*, are probably of that period; it was a Byzantine bell-tower, then a minaret, now a ruin. And here, confronting me, lie a few stones, that are all that remain of a pagan temple which became a Christian basilica and afterwards a mosque. In the fifth century Tisouros—this slumberous Bled-el-Adher—was a dependency of the Greek "Duke of Gafsa" (how strange it sounds!); Florentinus, its bishop, was executed by the king of the Vandals; Christian churches survived, side by side with mosques, as late as the fourteenth century. There seems to have been no great religious intolerance in those days.

They showed me a gold coin of the Emperor Gordian—the same who built the amphitheatre of El-Djem—which was found here, as well as some lamps and sculptured fragments of stone. Bruce speaks of cipollino columns; they are still to be seen, if you care to look for them, split up, since his time, to mend walls and doorsteps. Tozeur must have looked well enough under the later Empire.

And now, sand-heaps and a brood of young savages, shouting at their game.

It is long since these people knew the meaning of refined things, although some of the houses, their fronts decorated with gracious designs in brickwork, testify to a not extinct artistic feeling—the citizens once enjoyed a reputation for delicacy and love of letters. There is nothing like systematic misgovernment for degrading mankind, and I think it likely that the gradual fusion of the Arab and Berber races, so antagonistic in all their aspirations, may have helped to abrade the finer edges of both parent-stocks. But the native civilization was not remarkable at any time.

The climate, and then their religion, has made them hard and incurious; it is a land of uncompromising masculinity. The softer element—thanks to the Koran—has become non-existent, and you will look in vain for the creative-feminine, for those intermediate types of ambiguous, submerged sexuality, the constructive poets and dreamers, the men of imagination and women of will, that give to good society in the north its sweetness and **chatoyance**; for those "sports" and eccentrics who, among our lower classes, are centrifugal—perpetually tending to diverge in this or that direction. The native is pre-eminently centripetal. His life is reduced to its simplest physiological expression; that capacity of reflection, of forming suggestive and fruitful concepts, which lies at the bottom of every kind of progress or culture, has been sucked out of him by the sun and by Mahomet's teaching.

A land of violence, remorseless and relentless; the very beetles, so placid elsewhere, seem to have acquired a nervously virile temperament; they scurry about the sand at my feet with an air of rage and determination.

So I mused, while the game went on boisterously in the mellow light of sunset till, from some decaying minaret near by, there poured down a familiar long-drawn wail—the call to prayer. It was a golden hour among those mounds of sand, and I grew rather sad to think that I should never see the place again. How one longs to engrave certain memories upon the brain, to keep them untarnished and carry them about on one's journeyings, in all their freshness! The happiest life, seen in perspective, can hardly be better than a stringing together of such odd little moments.

Chapter XXII
THE DISMAL CHOTT

Hearing that there are few or no tourists in Nefta just now, I left Tozeur three days ago, an hour or so before sunrise.

This region, the Djerid, is all sand; an isthmus of sand thrust in between the two Chotts of Djerid and Rharsa; the oases ara scattered about the country, says some old writer, like the spots on a leopard's skin....

The air was keen, and I shivered on my mule, looking back often at the dark forest of Tozeur, where I had spent some happy days.

After about five miles of comfortable wading through soft sand, I became aware of a ghostly radiance that hovered over the pallid expanse of the Chott. Abruptly, with the splendour of a meteor, the morning star shot up. Then the sun's disk rose, more sedately, at the exact spot where Lucifer had shown the way; and climbing upwards, produced a spectacle for which I was not prepared.

For as it left the horizon, a counterfeit sun began to unroll itself from the true, as one might detach a petal from a rose; at first they clung together, but soon, with a wrench, parted company, and while the one soared aloft, the image remained below, weltering on the treacherous mere. For a short while the flaming phantasma lingered firm and orb-like, while the space between itself and reality grew to a hand's breadth; then slowly deliquesced. It gave a prolonged shiver and sank, convulsed, into the earth.

Light was diffused; the colour of daytime invaded the ground at our feet, flitting like some arterial rill through the dun spaces. Wonderful, this magic touch of awakening! It is the same swiftness of change as at sunset, when the desert folds itself to sleep, like some gorgeously palpitating flower, in the chill of nightfall; or rather, to use a metaphor which has often occurred to me, it hardens its features, crystallizing them into a stony mask, even as some face, once friendly, grows strangely indifferent in death.

My companion of this morning, who happened to be of a religious turn of mind, took the opportunity to glide off his beast and, standing a little apart, with his arms thrown through the reins to prevent the mule from straying, recited the dawn prayer. The noble gesticulations looked well on that bare sandy dune, in the face of the Chott.

As for myself, I thought of the old god Triton, who dwelt in yonder foul lake and showed some kindness to Jason, long ago, when his ships were entangled in the ooze; I thought of Tritogeneia, the savage, mud-born creature who, cast into the purifying crucible of Hellenic mythopoesis, emerged as bright-eyed Athene, mother of wisdom and domestic arts. The Amazon maidens of the country used to have combats in her honour with sticks and stones, and the fairest of them, decked in a panoply of Grecian armour, was conducted in a chariot about the lake. A fabled land! Here, they say, Poseidon was born, and Gorgo and Perseus, Medusa and Pegasus and other comely and wondrous shapes that have become familiar to us through Greek lore.

These folks of Atlantis "saw no dreams," but they studied astronomy and navigation; their priests may well have been those Druids whose temple-structures, the senams and cromlechs, have wandered from the Tripolitan frontier as far as the chilly coasts of Brittany, and Salisbury Plain, and Ultima Thule. And every day, as the sun passed over their heads, they saluted him not as the Giver of Life or Lord of Earth, but cursed him with imprecations long and loathsome, for his scorching fires.

Shaw, I believe, was the first to identify the Chotts with Lake Triton.

There were islands in this sea; the sacred isle of Phla, for instance, which the Spartans were commanded by an oracle to colonize, and whereon stood a temple to Aphrodite. There are islands to this day, great and small; one of them is called Faraoun—evidently an Egyptian name, for Egyptian influence was felt early in these regions; at Faraoun grows a peculiar kind of date which, we are told, an Egyptian army had left there. The waters of the pool touched Nefta, whose Kadi gave Tissot a description of a buried vessel which, from its shape, could be nothing but a "galere antique"—it was dismembered for fuel, and metal nails were found in its framework.

Movers is probably correct in seeking at Nefta the Biblical Naphtuhim of the generation of Noah: an Egyptian document speaks of it as the "land of Napit." Arabs have another theory of its origin. According to a chronicle preserved in the Nefta mosque, the founder of the town was Kostel, son of Sem, son of Noah; he called it Nefta because it was here that water boiled, for the first time, after the Deluge. The Romans called it Nepte, but, in confirmation of this old story, I observe that the Arabs of to-day invariably pronounce Nefta as *Nafta*. It is quite likely, too, that the name Hecatompylos, the city of a hundred gates, which has been applied to Gafsa, is a misreading for Hecatompolis, the land of those hundred cities which, they say, studded the shores of this great lake.

For it was a lake, or series of lakes, and nothing else; geological evidence is opposed to the supposition that the Chott country was ever a gulf of the Mediterranean within historical times—it was merely a chain of inland waters. And another surprising discovery has been made of late, namely, that these depressions lie at different levels and have, each of them, its own system of alimentation. This fact came to light between 1872 and 1883, when a number of studies were undertaken with a view to the restoration of this ancient Libyan Sea. Men of middle years will still remember the excitement produced by this scheme which originated with Tissot, though another name will for ever be associated with it, that of Roudaire, a man of science dominated by an obsession, who clung to this project with the blind faith of a martyr, his enthusiasm growing keener in proportion as the plan was proved to be futile, fantastic, fatuous. True, the great Lesseps had taken his part.

Desolation reigns on this morass of salt, where the life of man and beast, and even of plants and stones, faints away in mortal agony. Unnumbered multitudes of living creatures have sunk into its perfidious abysses. "A caravan of ours," says an Arab author, "had to cross the Chott one day; it was composed of a thousand baggage camels. Unfortunately one of the beasts strayed from the path, and all the others followed it. Nothing in the world could be swifter than the manner in which the crust yielded and engulphed them; then it became like what it was before, as if the thousand baggage camels had never existed." Yet it is traversed in several directions, and if you strain your eyes from these heights you can detect certain dusky lines that crawl in serpentine movement across the melancholy waste—caravan tracks to the south.

Unlike the living ocean, this withered one never smiles: it wears a hostile face. There is a charm, none the less—a charm that appeals to complex modern minds—in that picture of eternal, irremediable sterility. Its hue is ever-changing, as the light falls upon it; the plain, too, shifts up and down with mirage play, climbing sometimes into the horizon, or again sharply defined against it; often it resembles a milky river flowing between banks of mud. The surface is rarely lustrous, but of a velvety texture, like a banded agate, mouse-colour or liver-tinted, with paler streaks in between, of the dead whiteness of a sheet of paper; now and again there flash up livid coruscations that glister awhile like enamel or burnished steel, and then fade away. These are the fields of virgin salt which, when you cross them, are bright as purest Alpine snow, and may blind you temporarily with their dazzling glare. Viewed from these uplands, however, the ordered procession of horizontal bars stretching into infinity, their subdued coloration, fills the mind with a wave of deep peace.

Walking from Nefta to the Chott, you will reach, on the burning plain, a maraboutic shrine that might serve as an asylum for some conscience-stricken, malaria-proof penitent. They go well together, maraboutism and the Chott—two factors that make for barrenness in man and nature.

And Nefta is full of such shrines. Another one, for example, has been built into the very heart of the rustling palm forest; the water glides under its walls wherein sits the aged impostor who, unlike his amiable colleague at Tozeur, is too holy even to speak to unbelievers (you are permitted to gaze upon him through a grated window). Yet another one is the humble Sidi Murzouk, the negroes' sanctuary, among the sand-hills on the middle heights.

These are three representative types of a hundred, at least.

It is hard to say why the French foster these Arab maraboutic tendencies as opposed to the saner ideals of the Berber stock; perhaps they think it politic to *arabize* the older race in this and a few other particulars, though it signifies, almost invariably, a retrograde movement of civilization.

Of these pious folk the paradox is true that the best are the worst; those, that is, who do not expose themselves to ridicule or adverse criticism, whose good intentions are self-evident, who carry out to the letter the apostolic injunction of clothing the naked, feeding the hungry, and succouring the distressed. It is they who pander to all the worst qualities of the Arabs, improvident and incorrigible loafers, besides affording an asylum to every criminal; their *zaouiahs*, like our own mediaeval convents, are often enough mere menageries of deformed minds and bodies. As for the much-vaunted calm to be found within their walls, it is there, to be sure, together with certain other things—there and nowhere else, since the frantic religious passions, of which such monastic institutions are offshoots, have made peaceable living outside their walls an impossibility.

In a land where no one reads or writes or thinks or reasons, where dirt and insanity are regarded as marks of divine favour, how easy it is to acquire a reputation for holiness—(oral tradition alone can make a saint)—to turn the god-habit of your fellow-creatures into a profitable source of revenue: as easy as it was in Europe, in the days when we cherished such knaves and neurotic dreamers. Some of them are simple epileptics, verminous and importunate; others, shrewd worldly rogues who, having run away from home after a fit of discontent or homicide, cruise vaguely about Islamism for half a lifetime, and at last return, bearded venerables, to be stared at by their kinsfolk as portents, heaven-sent, because they have freighted themselves with a cargo of fond maxims such as "The World is Illusion: all Flesh is Vanity," and similar gnomic balderdash, the wisdom of the unlettered.

No wonder they despise what they call the world. For the real world, the cosmos of rational thought and action, has never existed for them. At Tangier, Mecca, Jerusalem or Timbuctu, they have sat eternally in the same coffee-houses or mosques, and listened eternally to the same theological chatterings; which accounts for a certain "family likeness" between all of these mentally starved creatures, who are nevertheless favoured of Allah so far as bodily comforts are concerned, inasmuch, as (if they play their cards correctly) money, wives, and lands pour down upon them till, in old age, they become so fuddled with homage and holy mumblings that they themselves cannot exactly remember whether they are humbugs or not: this, I take it, must be the culminating point, the *dernier mot*, of maraboutic enlightenment.

And beside these ten thousand impromptu saints that spring up daily out of the fertile soil of Arab imagination and poverty, every one of the descendants of Mahomet's daughter is a marabout, and all their children, male and female, in *saecula saeculorum*.

God alone, who numbers the stars, can keep count of their legions.

Chapter XXIII
THE GARDENS OF NEFTA

A person unacquainted with tropical vegetation would be amazed at the prodigality of the oasis of Nefta; in point of exuberance it is as superior to Tozeur as that to Gafsa. But the cathedral-like gravity of Tozeur is lacking; there is too much riot and opulence, too many voluptuous festoons and spears and spirals, a certain craving, so to speak, after the purely ornate: if Tozeur represents the decorative style of Louis Quatorze, this is assuredly Louis Seize. One great drawback is that the thick undergrowth often obstructs the view; and another, that you cannot walk about in all directions, as at Tozeur, because there is too much running water—perhaps one should say too few paths and bridges. For the last two days a sand-storm of unusual violence has been raging. On the ridges above the town one can hardly stand on one's feet; the grains fly upwards, over the crest of the hill, in blinding showers, mighty squadrons of them careering across the plain below. The landscape is involved in a dim, roseate twilight. But occasionally there comes a sickly radiance from behind the curtain of cloud that glimmers lustreless, like an incandescent lamp seen through a fog: it is the sun shining brightly in the pure regions of the upper air.

Here, under the trees, the wind is scarce felt, though you can perceive it by the fretful clashing of the palm branches overhead. And despite the storm there is a strange hush in the air, the hush of things to come, a sense of uneasiness; spring is upon us, buds are unfolding and waters draw up forcefully from a soil which seems to heave under one's very feet. It is a moment of throbbing intensity.

And the scirocco moans to these pangs of elemental gestation which man, the creature of earth, still darkly feels within him.

The ground is cultivated with mathematical parsimoniousness and divided into squares which made me think of the Roman *agrimensores*. But concerning this point, a civilized old native told me the following legend. Long ago, he said, these oases were wild jungles, and the few human creatures who lived near them little better than beasts. Then came a wise man who cut up and ploughed the watery district of Gafsa, Tozeur and Nefta; he planted trees and all the other growths useful to mankind; he divided the land into patches, led the water through them, and apportioned them among certain families—in short, he gave these oases their present shape, and did his work so well that up to this day no one has been able to suggest any improvements or to quarrel with his arrangement. The story interested me; it may be a variant of the old Hercules myth—it shows how much the Arabs, with their veneration for past heroes and prophets, and their sterile distrust in the possibility of any kind of progress, will believe.[3]

I will take this little credit to myself, that, unconvinced of my own explanation, I made further enquiries and learned that—allowing for the inevitable exaggeration—the man actually existed! His name was Ibn Shabbath; he was a kind of engineer-topographer who lived about the thirteenth century; he wrote a commentary, in three volumes, on some well-known Arabic geographical poem—a commentary which exists only in a few manuscript copies, one of which is preserved at the Grand Mosque in Tunis, and another, I am told, in the library of Monsieur de Fleury.

Yet the *deglat* palms which grow here in great abundance—the finest in the world—with their lower leaves pendent, sere and yellow; the figs, lemons, apricots and pomegranates clustering in savage meshes of unpruned boughs among which the vine, likewise unkempt, writhes and clambers liana-fashion, in crazy convolutions—all these things conspire to give to certain parts of the oasis, notwithstanding its high cultivation, a bearded, primeval look. The palms, particularly the young ones, are assiduously tended and groomed by half-naked gardeners who labour in the moist earth by relays, day and night.

What nights of brooding stillness in summer, under the palms, when those leaves hang motionless in the steaming vapour as though carved out of bronze, while the surrounding desert exhales the fiery emanations of noontide, often 135

---

3 It shows, also, that one cannot be too careful what one writes.

degrees in the shade. For the heat of Nefta is hellish. One might think that the inhabitants, whom Bertholon holds to be descendants, somewhat remote, of the old marrow-sucking, grandmother-devouring Neanderthal folk, would have become placid by this time; that all harshness must have been boiled out of them. Far from it! The faces that one sees are less friendly than those at Tozeur, and they were noted, in former days, for their vehemence in religious matters. I am sorry to hear it, but not surprised. The arts and other fair flowerings of the human mind may succumb to fierce climates, but theological zeal is one of those things which no extremes of temperature can subdue; it thrives equally well at the Poles or Equator, like that "Brown or Hanoverian rat" which Charles Waterton—a glorious old zealot himself—so cordially detested.

There are eight Europeans here, and thirteen thousand natives: I should not care to be in Nefta on the day when the Senoussi are to realize their long-deferred hopes. All the same, it is a relief not to hear the eternal gossip of employes or to see the soldiers loitering at street corners, like dressed-up chimpanzees. The better class of natives are sometimes of an astonishing immaculate cleanliness from head to foot; they are often remarkably handsome. The traveller Temple was struck, at Nefta, with the beauty of its "desert nymphs, whose eyes are all fire and brilliancy," and he might have said the same of the boys.

But I observe a defect in the eyes of all Arabs, namely, that they seem to be unable to utilize them as a means of conveying thoughts; they have no eye language, even among each other, and must express by words or by some gesture what other people can make clear with a glance. The best-looking youth or maiden has eyes which, beautiful as they are, might be those of a stuffed cow for all the expression they emit. They cannot even wink.

From the rising ground at the back of Nefta you look down into a circular vale of immoderate plant-luxuriance, a never-ending delight of the eye; the French call it by the appropriate name of "la corbeille." Here the springs issue—152 of them—from under steep walls of sand; they form glad pools of blue and green that mirror the foliage with impeccable truthfulness and then, after coursing in distracted filaments about the "corbeille," join their waters and speed downhill towards the oasis, a narrow belt of trees running along either side. This marvellous palm-embroidered rift sunders Nefta, seated on the arid sand-hills overhead, into two distinct towns or settlements. The eye follows the stream as far as the low-lying plantations and into the Chott beyond, resting at last upon the violet haze of its mysterious southern shores.

Visible from here are also certain mounds at the eastern extremity of the oasis, near the Chott; they are marked on the map as "ruins of Zafrana." What this Zafrana was, or how it comes to have a name resembling that of a small Sicilian village, I cannot tell; thither, at all events, I bent my steps, having heard that ancient coins, as well as lamps, had been found here. So far as I can make out there is only pottery on this site, and none of it pre-Mohammedan; if a city ever stood here it has been completely entombed, or torn into shreds by the wind, the flying sands, and the heat. Nefta itself, built of soft loam, would crumble away in briefest time if left unrepaired. The acute Guerin was not more successful than myself at Zafrana, nor was Maltzan.

This being the most exposed corner of the oasis, the *tabias* have grown to a fine size; I climbed over the inner one, which must be ten yards high and at least twenty in breadth. From its summit one perceives distant forms of ruinous buildings rising up in the Tozeur direction, on the slope which inclines to the Chott. Was this, perhaps, Zafrana?

No. Riding up to them, I found they were merely turret-like eminences of hard bluish clay, the carapace of the desert, which the wind has carved into quaint semblances of human dwellings. In the evening light they catch the last rays of the sun and shine like diaphanous spectres upon the darkened ground, but at sunrise, when the yellow sands sparkle with light, they tower up grim and menacing: a mournful, ghoul-haunted region, like those veritable townships of the past, Dougga, Timgad and the rest of them, standing all forlorn in their African desolation.

Whoever has visited such sites will understand the impression they conveyed to men of simpler ages. He will realize how they must have inflamed the phantasy of those wandering mediaeval Arabs who could make no distinction, in this respect, between the works of man and those of nature, nor bring themselves to believe that such titanic structures were reared by human hands or for any human purpose— were otherwise than an illusion, or a natural incongruity. That amphitheatre of El-Djem, for example, visible for leagues in the solitude around—what more apt to become a true mountain of wondrous shape, the haunt of some Ifrit imprisoned in its cup or soaring thence, a pillar of cloud, into the zenith?

These are the ruins whose report was carried to Bagdhad by those early caravan traders, and there woven into the flowery tapestries of the "Arabian Nights"—nightmare cities, rising like an enchantment out of the desert sand; bereft of the voices and footsteps of men, but teeming with hoarded treasure and graven images of gods that gaze down, inscrutable and sternly resplendent, upon the wanderer who, stumbling fearfully through a labyrinth of silent halls, suddenly encounters, in demon-guarded chamber, some ensorcelled maiden, frozen to stone.

Chapter XXIV
NEFTA AND ITS FUTURE

There are cities in the East where, from ramparts that support fairy-like palaces—complicated assemblages of courts and plashing fountains and cool chambers through which the breeze wanders in an artificial twilight of marble screens pierced so craftily, one might think them a flowing drapery of lace-work—where, from such wizard creations of Oriental pomp, you glance down and behold, stretched at your feet, a burning waste of sand. A fine incentive to the luxurious imagination of a tyrant, this contrast, that has all the glamour of a dream....

But such abrupt transitions are not the rule. Midway between the pulsating town-life and the desert there lies, mostly, a sinister extra-mural region, a region of gaping walls and potsherds, where the asphodel shoot up to monstrous tufts and the fallacious colocynth, the wild melon, scatters its globes of bitter gold. For it is in the nature of Orientals that their habitations should surround themselves with a girdle of corrupting things, gruesome and yet fascinating: a Browning might have grown enamoured of its macabre spell.

No European cares to linger about these precincts after dusk; here lie the dead, in thick-strewn graves; here the jackal roams at night—it thrusts its pointed snout through the ephemeral masonry of townsmen's tombs or scratches downward within the ring of stones that mark some poor bedouin's corpse, to take toll of the carrion horrors beneath; so you may find many graves rifled. And if you come by day you will probably see, crouching among the ruins, certain old men, pariahs, animated lumps of dirt and rags. They are so uncouth and unclean, so utterly non-human, that one wonders whether they are really of the sons of Adam, and not rather goblins, or possibly some freak, some ill-natured jest on the part of the vegetable or mineral kingdoms. Day after day they come and burrow for orts among the dust-heaps, or brood motionless in the sunshine, or trace cabalistic signs with their fingers in the sand—the future, they tell you, can be unriddled out of its cascade-like movements.

It is one of the complaints of sentimentalists that the French are abolishing these picturesque Arab cemeteries in Tunisia; combining firmness with a great deal of tact, they insidiously appropriate these sanctified premises and deck them with timber as a solace for coming generations. Let them go! The undiluted Orient is still wide enough; and no one will appreciate the metamorphosis more than the native citizens themselves, who love, above all things, to play about and idle in the shade of trees; perhaps, in the course of time, they will realize that not only Allah, but also man, is able to plant and take care of them. Your Arab often has a love of nature which is none the worse for being wholly unconscious.

At Nefta there is no impure region, properly so called. The searching sunbeams and the winds are inimical to all the lush concomitants of decay; the sand also plays its part; so every dead dog, and every dead camel, arrests the flying grains and is straightway interred—transformed into a hillock, trivial but sanitary.

There are tombs, of course, tombs galore; but what strikes one most are the numerous shrines erected to saints alive or dead, of which I have already spoken.

You will do well to visit the Christian cemetery. It lies on an eminence above the town and is almost buried under deep waves of sand, which have risen to the summit of the surrounding walls and drowned the three graves, all but their tall stones that emerge above the flood. One of them is that of a ***controlleur*** of the district who died at his post while combating a cholera epidemic—there may be more of them, for aught I know, submerged beneath the drift.

It is surely in the interests of French prestige to pay a few francs for the cleansing of such a place in a land where, as conquerors, they live on a pedestal and are to assert their superiority in every way. It will be long ere Arabs can appreciate French art and science, but they understand visible trifles of this kind, and, conversing with them, I have found that, like many simple-minded people, they are disposed to contrast unfavourably their own burial-grounds with our trim method of sepulture, which assures to the defunct a few more years of apparent respect, while flattering the vanity of the living. To a sensitive Christian this cemetery of Nefta must be a sad and a scandalous sight; no humble nomad's tomb on the bleak hillside is more neglected than these memorials to his fellow-believers who have died, far from their homes, under the flaming sun of Africa.

From this point you can see the tail-end of the oasis. It lies in the Zafrana region, and is the worst nourished. This, I suppose, is inevitable; the gardens must be continually moving—moving away from the Chott towards their vital sources, which now lie under a respectable precipice of sand. It is hard to believe that the present site of the fountains is what one might call the natural, aboriginal one. I imagine that the cultivators, in the course of ages, must have tracked the element and followed it up, as a terrier will pursue a rabbit in its burrow, planting trees in proportion as they laid bare its once subterranean bed. Thus, the supply of liquid being constant, the oasis is impelled to wander in the direction of its springs; the more you add to the head, the shorter grows the tail. In prehistoric days, maybe, the water gushed out somewhere near the Chott; the charming depression of the "corbeille" is perhaps the work of human hands.

The same has struck me at Tozeur, which also marches horizontally away from its termination. An exquisite corbeille could be manufactured here; all the elements are present; it only requires a few thousand years of labour. And what are they, in a land like this?

And the oases are undergoing another and more curious progression—downwards. Strange to think that, while towns and villages rise higher every year, these gardens are slowly descending into the depths; they are already far below the circumambient desert, though not so deeply sunk as the verdant, crater-like depressions of some parts of Africa. For it stands to reason that as the stream-beds become excavated more and more—and this is what has brought them to their present position—the groves must irrevocably follow suit, since water escapes at the lowest level, while trees cannot be suspended in air. Supposing the system of dams, which now force the liquid to keep to a certain plane, fell into disuse, how would it end?

The imagination of an Edgar Poe might picture these Nefta gardens as the reverse of those of Semiramis—sunk, that is, further into the profundities of the earth than the already existing Sahara plantations—with this difference, that here, to obviate infiltration from the ooze of the Chott, sturdy walls must enclose them.

Ages pass, and still the groves descend, while the defences grow so stout and high that, viewed from above, the palms down there, in that deep funnel, look like puny vegetables, and men like ants. And still they descend.... One day the pale population engaged in tilling this shadowy paradise will be horrified to perceive, in their encircling bulwarks, rents and crevices that ooze forth ominous jets of mud. The damage is hastily repaired, but the cracks appear once more, and, widening imperceptibly at first, soon burst asunder and admit, from every side, a wrinkled flood of slime which closes with sullen murmur over the site of the drowned oasis.

Or if the wells dried up? One of those geological displacements that have taken place in past times would suffice to wipe out the memory of this town—the palms would wither, the clay-built houses melt into the earth whence they arose.

Meanwhile, perched on the last wave of an ocean of shining sand, Nefta sits in immemorial contemplation of the desert and vividly green oasis which flows, like a grand and luminous river, into the very heart of its flat dwellings. There is a note of passionate solemnity about the place. All too soon, I fear, the railway to Tozeur will have done its work; dusty boulevards, white bungalows, eucalyptus trees and **bureaux de monopoles** will profane its strangely wonderful beauty, its virginal monotone of golden grey. Nefta will become a neurasthenic demi-mondaine, like Biskra.

Such, at least, is the prognosis.

But one is apt to forget on how precarious a tenure these gardens are held, with the hungry desert gnawing ceaselessly at their outskirts; for the desert is hungry and yet patient; it has devoured sundry oases by simply waiting till man is preoccupied with other matters. And how rare they are, these specks of green, these fountains in the sand—rare as the smiles in a lifetime of woe! Beyond and all around lies a grave and ungracious land, the land of the lawless, fanatical wanderers.

Those Romans and heathen Berbers, tillers of the soil, had remained in contact with phenomena; unconcerned, relatively speaking, with the affairs of the next world, they attained a passable degree of civilization in this one. But your pastoral Arab scorns a knowledge of general mundane principles. His life is a series of disconnected happenings which must be enjoyed or endured; he is incapable of reading aright the past or present, because he asks himself *why?* instead of *how?* Whoever despises the investigation of secondary causes is a menace to his fellow-creatures.

Face to face with infinities, man disencumbers himself. Those abysmal desert-silences, those spaces of scintillating rock and sand-dune over which the eye roams and vainly seeks a point of repose, quicken his animal perception; he stands alone and must think for himself—and so far good. But while discarding much that seems inconsiderable before such wide and splendid horizons, this nomad loads himself with the incubus of dream-states; while standing alone, he grows into a ferocious brigand. Poets call him romantic, but politicians are puzzled what to do with a being who to a senile mysticism joins the peevish destructiveness of a child.

It is an almost universal fallacy to blame the desert for this state of affairs; to insinuate, for example, that even as it disintegrates the mountains into sand, so it decomposes the intellectual fabric of mankind, his synthesizing faculty, into its primordial elements of ecstasy and emotionalism. This is merely reaction: the desert's revenge. For we now know a little something of the condition of old Arabia and Africa in the days ere these ardent shepherds appeared on the scene, with their crude and chaotic monotheism. The desert has not made the Arab, any more than it made the Berber. It would be considerably nearer the truth to reverse the proposition: to say that the evils which now afflict Northern Africa, its physical abandonment, its social and economical decay, are the work of that ideal Arab, the man of Mecca. Mahomet is the desert-maker.

THE END

www.bookjungle.com *email: sales@bookjungle.com fax: 630-214-0564 mail: Book Jungle PO Box 2226 Champaign, IL 61825*

The Codes Of Hammurabi And Moses
W. W. Davies

QTY

The discovery of the Hammurabi Code is one of the greatest achievements of archaeology, and is of paramount interest, not only to the student of the Bible, but also to all those interested in ancient history...

Religion   **ISBN:** *1-59462-338-4*   **Pages:** 132
 MSRP $12.95

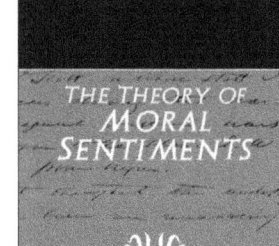

The Theory of Moral Sentiments
Adam Smith

QTY

This work from 1749. contains original theories of conscience amd moral judgment and it is the foundation for systemof morals.

Philosophy   **ISBN:** *1-59462-777-0*   **Pages:** 536
 MSRP $19.95

Jessica's First Prayer
Hesba Stretton

QTY

In a screened and secluded corner of one of the many railway-bridges which span the streets of London there could be seen a few years ago, from five o'clock every morning until half past eight, a tidily set-out coffee-stall, consisting of a trestle and board, upon which stood two large tin cans, with a small fire of charcoal burning under each so as to keep the coffee boiling during the early hours of the morning when the work-people were thronging into the city on their way to their daily toil...

Childrens   **ISBN:** *1-59462-373-2*   **Pages:** 84
 MSRP $9.95

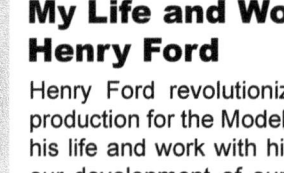

My Life and Work
Henry Ford

QTY

Henry Ford revolutionized the world with his implementation of mass production for the Model T automobile. Gain valuable business insight into his life and work with his own auto-biography... "We have only started on our development of our country we have not as yet, with all our talk of wonderful progress, done more than scratch the surface. The progress has been wonderful enough but..."

Biographies/   **ISBN:** *1-59462-198-5*   **Pages:** 300
 MSRP $21.95

www.bookjungle.com *email: sales@bookjungle.com fax: 630-214-0564 mail: Book Jungle PO Box 2226 Champaign, IL 61825*

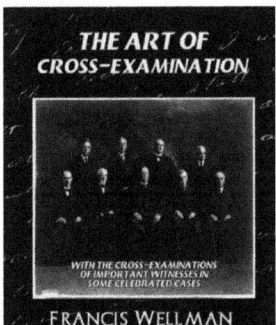

The Art of Cross-Examination
Francis Wellman

QTY

I presume it is the experience of every author, after his first book is published upon an important subject, to be almost overwhelmed with a wealth of ideas and illustrations which could readily have been included in his book, and which to his own mind, at least, seem to make a second edition inevitable. Such certainly was the case with me; and when the first edition had reached its sixth impression in five months, I rejoiced to learn that it seemed to my publishers that the book had met with a sufficiently favorable reception to justify a second and considerably enlarged edition. ..

Pages:412

Reference   ISBN: *1-59462-647-2*   *MSRP $19.95*

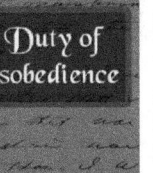

On the Duty of Civil Disobedience
Henry David Thoreau

QTY

Thoreau wrote his famous essay, On the Duty of Civil Disobedience, as a protest against an unjust but popular war and the immoral but popular institution of slave-owning. He did more than write—he declined to pay his taxes, and was hauled off to gaol in consequence. Who can say how much this refusal of his hastened the end of the war and of slavery ?

Law   ISBN: *1-59462-747-9*   **Pages:48**
MSRP $7.45

Dream Psychology Psychoanalysis for Beginners
Sigmund Freud

QTY

Sigmund Freud, born Sigismund Schlomo Freud (May 6, 1856 - September 23, 1939), was a Jewish-Austrian neurologist and psychiatrist who co-founded the psychoanalytic school of psychology. Freud is best known for his theories of the unconscious mind, especially involving the mechanism of repression; his redefinition of sexual desire as mobile and directed towards a wide variety of objects; and his therapeutic techniques, especially his understanding of transference in the therapeutic relationship and the presumed value of dreams as sources of insight into unconscious desires.

Pages:196

Psychology   ISBN: *1-59462-905-6*   *MSRP $15.45*

The Miracle of Right Thought
Orison Swett Marden

QTY

Believe with all of your heart that you will do what you were made to do. When the mind has once formed the habit of holding cheerful, happy, prosperous pictures, it will not be easy to form the opposite habit. It does not matter how improbable or how far away this realization may see, or how dark the prospects may be, if we visualize them as best we can, as vividly as possible, hold tenaciously to them and vigorously struggle to attain them, they will gradually become actualized, realized in the life. But a desire, a longing without endeavor, a yearning abandoned or held indifferently will vanish without realization.

Pages:360

Self Help   ISBN: *1-59462-644-8*   *MSRP $25.45*

www.bookjungle.com email: sales@bookjungle.com fax: 630-214-0564 mail: Book Jungle PO Box 2226 Champaign, IL 61825

QTY

	Title	ISBN	Price
☐	**The Rosicrucian Cosmo-Conception Mystic Christianity** by *Max Heindel*	ISBN: 1-59462-188-8	$38.95
	The Rosicrucian Cosmo-conception is not dogmatic, neither does it appeal to any other authority than the reason of the student. It is: not controversial, but is: sent forth in the, hope that it may help to clear...	New Age/Religion Pages 646	
☐	**Abandonment To Divine Providence** by *Jean-Pierre de Caussade*	ISBN: 1-59462-228-0	$25.95
	"The Rev. Jean Pierre de Caussade was one of the most remarkable spiritual writers of the Society of Jesus in France in the 18th Century. His death took place at Toulouse in 1751. His works have gone through many editions and have been republished...	Inspirational/Religion Pages 400	
☐	**Mental Chemistry** by *Charles Haanel*	ISBN: 1-59462-192-6	$23.95
	Mental Chemistry allows the change of material conditions by combining and appropriately utilizing the power of the mind. Much like applied chemistry creates something new and unique out of careful combinations of chemicals the mastery of mental chemistry...	New Age Pages 354	
☐	**The Letters of Robert Browning and Elizabeth Barret Barrett 1845-1846 vol II** by *Robert Browning* and *Elizabeth Barrett*	ISBN: 1-59462-193-4	$35.95
		Biographies Pages 596	
☐	**Gleanings In Genesis (volume I)** by *Arthur W. Pink*	ISBN: 1-59462-130-6	$27.45
	Appropriately has Genesis been termed "the seed plot of the Bible" for in it we have, in germ form, almost all of the great doctrines which are afterwards fully developed in the books of Scripture which follow...	Religion/Inspirational Pages 420	
☐	**The Master Key** by *L. W. de Laurence*	ISBN: 1-59462-001-6	$30.95
	In no branch of human knowledge has there been a more lively increase of the spirit of research during the past few years than in the study of Psychology, Concentration and Mental Discipline. The requests for authentic lessons in Thought Control, Mental Discipline and...	New Age/Business Pages 422	
☐	**The Lesser Key Of Solomon Goetia** by *L. W. de Laurence*	ISBN: 1-59462-092-X	$9.95
	This translation of the first book of the "Lernegton" which is now for the first time made accessible to students of Talismanic Magic was done, after careful collation and edition, from numerous Ancient Manuscripts in Hebrew, Latin, and French...	New Age/Occult Pages 92	
☐	**Rubaiyat Of Omar Khayyam** by *Edward Fitzgerald*	ISBN:1-59462-332-5	$13.95
	Edward Fitzgerald, whom the world has already learned, in spite of his own efforts to remain within the shadow of anonymity, to look upon as one of the rarest poets of the century, was born at Bredfield, in Suffolk, on the 31st of March, 1809. He was the third son of John Purcell...	Music Pages 172	
☐	**Ancient Law** by *Henry Maine*	ISBN: 1-59462-128-4	$29.95
	The chief object of the following pages is to indicate some of the earliest ideas of mankind, as they are reflected in Ancient Law, and to point out the relation of those ideas to modern thought.	Religiom/History Pages 452	
☐	**Far-Away Stories** by *William J. Locke*	ISBN: 1-59462-129-2	$19.45
	"Good wine needs no bush, but a collection of mixed vintages does. And this book is just such a collection. Some of the stories I do not want to remain buried for ever in the museum files of dead magazine-numbers an author's not unpardonable vanity..."	Fiction Pages 272	
☐	**Life of David Crockett** by *David Crockett*	ISBN: 1-59462-250-7	$27.45
	"Colonel David Crockett was one of the most remarkable men of the times in which he lived. Born in humble life, but gifted with a strong will, an indomitable courage, and unremitting perseverance...	Biographies/New Age Pages 424	
☐	**Lip-Reading** by *Edward Nitchie*	ISBN: 1-59462-206-X	$25.95
	Edward B. Nitchie, founder of the New York School for the Hard of Hearing, now the Nitchie School of Lip-Reading, Inc, wrote "LIP-READING Principles and Practice". The development and perfecting of this meritorious work on lip-reading was an undertaking...	How-to Pages 400	
☐	**A Handbook of Suggestive Therapeutics, Applied Hypnotism, Psychic Science** by *Henry Munro*	ISBN: 1-59462-214-0	$24.95
		Health/New Age/Health/Self-help Pages 376	
☐	**A Doll's House: and Two Other Plays** by *Henrik Ibsen*	ISBN: 1-59462-112-8	$19.95
	Henrik Ibsen created this classic when in revolutionary 1848 Rome. Introducing some striking concepts in playwriting for the realist genre, this play has been studied the world over.	Fiction/Classics/Plays 308	
☐	**The Light of Asia** by *sir Edwin Arnold*	ISBN: 1-59462-204-3	$13.95
	In this poetic masterpiece, Edwin Arnold describes the life and teachings of Buddha. The man who was to become known as Buddha to the world was born as Prince Gautama of India but he rejected the worldly riches and abandoned the reigns of power when...	Religion/History/Biographies Pages 170	
☐	**The Complete Works of Guy de Maupassant** by *Guy de Maupassant*	ISBN: 1-59462-157-8	$16.95
	"For days and days, nights and nights, I had dreamed of that first kiss which was to consecrate our engagement, and I knew not on what spot I should put my lips..."	Fiction/Classics Pages 240	
☐	**The Art of Cross-Examination** by *Francis L. Wellman*	ISBN: 1-59462-309-0	$26.95
	Written by a renowned trial lawyer, Wellman imparts his experience and uses case studies to explain how to use psychology to extract desired information through questioning.	How-to/Science/Reference Pages 408	
☐	**Answered or Unanswered?** by *Louisa Vaughan*	ISBN: 1-59462-248-5	$10.95
	Miracles of Faith in China	Religion Pages 112	
☐	**The Edinburgh Lectures on Mental Science (1909)** by *Thomas*	ISBN: 1-59462-008-3	$11.95
	This book contains the substance of a course of lectures recently given by the writer in the Queen Street Hall, Edinburgh. Its purpose is to indicate the Natural Principles governing the relation between Mental Action and Material Conditions...	New Age/Psychology Pages 148	
☐	**Ayesha** by *H. Rider Haggard*	ISBN: 1-59462-301-5	$24.95
	Verily and indeed it is the unexpected that happens! Probably if there was one person upon the earth from whom the Editor of this, and of a certain previous history, did not expect to hear again...	Classics Pages 380	
☐	**Ayala's Angel** by *Anthony Trollope*	ISBN: 1-59462-352-X	$29.95
	The two girls were both pretty, but Lucy who was twenty-one who supposed to be simple and comparatively unattractive, whereas Ayala was credited, as her Bombwhat romantic name might show, with poetic charm and a taste for romance. Ayala when her father died was nineteen...	Fiction Pages 484	
☐	**The American Commonwealth** by *James Bryce*	ISBN: 1-59462-286-8	$34.45
	An interpretation of American democratic political theory. It examines political mechanics and society from the perspective of Scotsman James Bryce	Politics Pages 572	
☐	**Stories of the Pilgrims** by *Margaret P. Pumphrey*	ISBN: 1-59462-116-0	$17.95
	This book explores pilgrims religious oppression in England as well as their escape to Holland and eventual crossing to America on the Mayflower, and their early days in New England...	History Pages 268	

www.bookjungle.com *email: sales@bookjungle.com fax: 630-214-0564 mail: Book Jungle PO Box 2226 Champaign, IL 61825*

QTY

The Fasting Cure *by Sinclair Upton*   ISBN: *1-59462-222-1* **$13.95**
In the Cosmopolitan Magazine for May, 1910, and in the Contemporary Review (London) for April, 1910, I published an article dealing with my experiences in fasting. I have written a great many magazine articles, but never one which attracted so much attention... New Age/Self Help/Health Pages 164

Hebrew Astrology *by Sepharial*   ISBN: *1-59462-308-2* **$13.45**
In these days of advanced thinking it is a matter of common observation that we have left many of the old landmarks behind and that we are now pressing forward to greater heights and to a wider horizon than that which represented the mind-content of our progenitors... Astrology Pages 144

Thought Vibration or The Law of Attraction in the Thought World   ISBN: *1-59462-127-6* **$12.95**
by William Walker Atkinson   Psychology/Religion Pages 144

Optimism *by Helen Keller*   ISBN: *1-59462-108-X* **$15.95**
Helen Keller was blind, deaf, and mute since 19 months old, yet famously learned how to overcome these handicaps, communicate with the world, and spread her lectures promoting optimism. An inspiring read for everyone... Biographies/Inspirational Pages 84

Sara Crewe *by Frances Burnett*   ISBN: *1-59462-360-0* **$9.45**
In the first place, Miss Minchin lived in London. Her home was a large, dull, tall one, in a large, dull square, where all the houses were alike, and all the sparrows were alike, and where all the door-knockers made the same heavy sound... Childrens/Classic Pages 88

The Autobiography of Benjamin Franklin *by Benjamin Franklin*   ISBN: *1-59462-135-7* **$24.95**
The Autobiography of Benjamin Franklin has probably been more extensively read than any other American historical work, and no other book of its kind has had such ups and downs of fortune. Franklin lived for many years in England, where he was agent... Biographies/History Pages 332

Name	
Email	
Telephone	
Address	
City, State ZIP	

☐ Credit Card   ☐ Check / Money Order

Credit Card Number	
Expiration Date	
Signature	

Please Mail to: Book Jungle
PO Box 2226
Champaign, IL 61825
or Fax to: 630-214-0564

ORDERING INFORMATION

web: *www.bookjungle.com*
email: *sales@bookjungle.com*
fax: *630-214-0564*
mail: *Book Jungle PO Box 2226 Champaign, IL 61825*
or PayPal *to sales@bookjungle.com*

Please contact us for bulk discounts

DIRECT-ORDER TERMS

**20% Discount if You Order
Two or More Books**
Free Domestic Shipping!
Accepted: Master Card, Visa,
Discover, American Express

www.ingramcontent.com/pod-product-compliance
Lightning Source LLC
Chambersburg PA
CBHW080514110426
42742CB00017B/3114